Quick Reference Guide™

D1806010

DDC

Works 3
for Windows™

Maria Reidelbach

DDC Publishing

14 East 38 St New York, NY 10016

First Dictation Disc Printing
Catalog No. O-WKW3

ISBN: 1-56243-141-2

10   9   8   7   6   5   4   3

Printed in the United States of America

INTRODUCTION

Welcome to the **DDC Quick Reference Guide for Works 3 for Windows.** This guide will save you hours of searching through technical manuals.

You can easily perform a desired action by following the step-by-step instructions

Author:	**Maria Reidelbach**
Editor:	**Don Gosselin**
Technical Editing and Consulting:	**Don Gosselin**
Layout and Design:	**Chassman Graphics**

TABLE OF CONTENTS

(continued...)

TABLE OF CONTENTS (continued)

(continued...)

TABLE OF CONTENTS (continued)

(continued...)

V

TABLE OF CONTENTS (continued)

(continued...)

vi

TABLE OF CONTENTS (continued)

Works Basics

START WORKS AND CREATE A NEW DOCUMENT, SPREADSHEET, OR DATABASE FILE

– FROM WINDOW GROUP–

Microsoft
Works

1. Double-click Works program item ....

If you have just installed Works and the Welcome dialog box appears:

Click **Skip Welcome Screen**...................................... S

The Startup dialog box appears:

2. Choose one of the following options:

   • Click **Word Processor** button...............................

     OR

     Press... W

   • Click **Spreadsheet** button ....

     OR

     Press... S

   • Click **Database** button..

     OR

   • Press... D

(continued...)

2

WORKS BASIC (continued)

- Click **Communications** button ....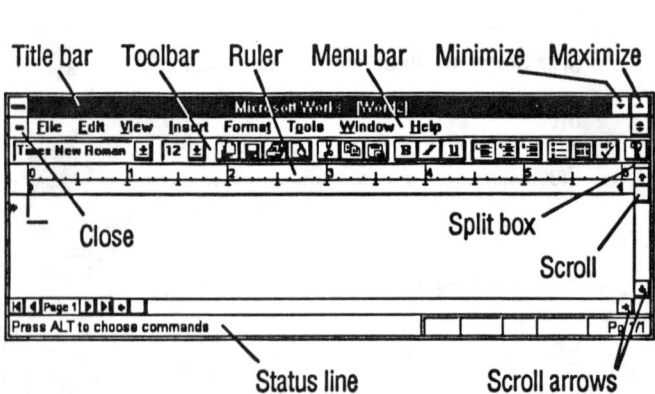

  OR

- Press... 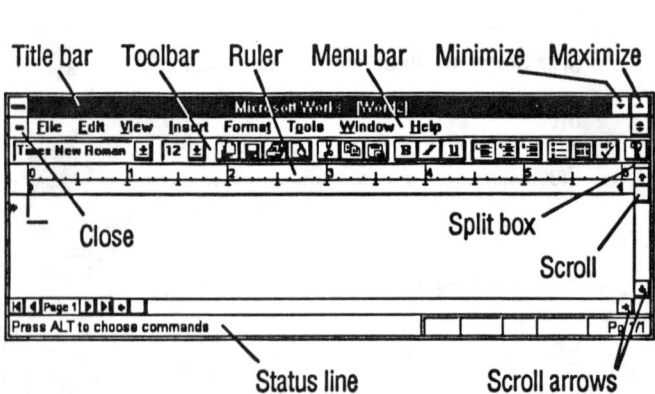 S

If Microsoft Works window appears:

a. Click **File** .... **Alt** + **F**

b. Click **Create New File** .... **N**

3. Choose desired file type from the following options:

   - **Word Processor** button.................................. **W**

   - **Spreadsheet** button .... **S**

   - **Database** button .... **D**

   - **Communications** button .... **C**

– THE WORKS WINDOW –

Title bar Toolbar Ruler Menu bar Minimize Maximize

Close

Split box

Scroll

Status line

Scroll arrows

CREATE NEW FILE WHEN WORKS IS ALREADY STARTED

1. Click **Startup** button on toolbar .... 🗗

   OR

   a. Click **File** menu .... Alt + F

   b. Click **Create New File** .... N

2. Open desired file type:

   • Click **Word Processor** button .... 📝

      OR

      Press .... W

   • Click **Spreadsheet** button .... 📊

      OR

      Press .... S

   • Click **Database** button .... 📇

      OR

      Press .... D

   • Click **Communications** button .... 🖥

      OR

      Press C

4

OPEN EXISTING FILE

–FROM STARTUP WINDOW–

1. Click **Open An Existing Document** button...... `Open An Existing Document`

   OR

   a. Click **File** menu... `Alt` + `F`

   b. Click **Open Existing File**.................................. `O`

2. Select desired filename from **File Name** list box.

   To select file from different drive:

   a. Choose **Drives** .... `⬇`

   b. Choose desired drive.

   c. Choose desired file from **Filename** list box.

   To select file from different directory:

   a. Double-click desired directory name in **Directories** list box.

   b. Choose desired file from **File Name** list box.

OPEN RECENTLY USED FILES

–FROM STARTUP WINDOW –

Double-click desired file name in **Recently used files** list box.

OR

a. Press .... `R`

b. Press .... `⬇`
   repeatedly to select desired file name.

c. Press .... `↵`

SAVE FILES

Save File for First Time

1. Click **F**ile menu .... `Alt` + `F`

2. Click **S**ave .... `S`

3. Type filename .... *filename*
   in **File Name** text box.

4. Click **OK** .... `Enter`

Save File While at Work on it

1. Click **F**ile menu .... `Alt` + `F`

2. Click **S**ave .... `S`

Save Second Copy of File

1. Click **F**ile menu .... `Alt` + `F`

2. Click **Save As** .... `A`

3. Type a filename in the **File Name** text box.

4. Click **OK** .... `Enter`

CLOSE FILE

1. Click **F**ile menu .... `Alt` + `F`

2. Click **C**lose .... `C`

3. Click **Y**es .... `Y`
   to save changes and close file.

   If saving document for first time:

   a. Type name .... *name*
      in **File Name** text box of **Save As** dialog box.

(continued...)

6

CLOSE FILE (continued)

   b. Click **OK**.. `Enter`

   OR

   Click **No** .... `N`
   to discard changes and close file.

   Click **Cancel**....................................... `Esc`
   to return to document.

CLOSE FILES AND EXIT WORKS

1. Click **File** menu............................ `Alt` + `F`

2. Click **Exit**... `X`

3. Click **Yes**... `Y`
   to save changes and close each file.

If any open files have never been saved:

1. Type name ....*name*
   in the **File Name** text box .

2. Click **OK**....................................... `Enter`

OR

Click **No** .... `N`
to discard changes and close each file.

OR

Click **Cancel** .... `Esc`
to return to documents.

UNDO CHANGE

NOTE: *Everyone makes mistakes! In most cases, you may undo your most recent click or keystrokes.*

Press .... `Ctrl` + `Z`

OR

a. Click **E**dit menu.................................... `Alt` + `E`

b. Click **U**ndo .... `U`

NOTE: *The **Undo** choice may vary depending on what edits have recently been done.*

Redo Changed Editing

Allows you to redo the edit back to its original form, if you don't like the change UNDO made.

Press .... `Ctrl` + `Z`

OR

a. Click **E**dit menu.................................... `Alt` + `E`

b. Click **R**edo Editing .... `R`

VIEW TWO PARTS OF FILE

1. Point to split box (see page 2).

2. Click and drag box to desired location.

To remove split:

Double-click split bar.

Insert, Move or Remove Split

1. Click **W**indow menu .... `Alt` + `W`

2. Click **S**plit.. `S`

(continued...)

8

INSERT MOVE OR REMOVE SPLIT (continued)

3. Press .... `↑` `←` `↓` `→`

    OR

    Drag split bar with mouse.

4. Press .... `Enter`

Move Between Panes of Split Window

Click in desired pane.

OR

Press .... `Alt` + `F6`

VIEW OR HIDE TOOLBAR

1. Click **View** menu .... `Alt` + `V`

2. Click **Toolbar** .... `B`
    to select (✓)or deselect.

Add or Remove Toolbar Button

1. Click **Tools** menu .... `Alt` + `O`

2. Click **Customize Toolbar** .... `U`

3. Choose option from **Categories** list .... `PgDn`

4. Click button to see description of function below.

5. Drag desired button to toolbar.

6. Repeat step 5 to add additional buttons.

7. To remove button, click and drag it from the toolbar.

8. Click **OK** .... `Enter`

TEMPLATES

NOTE: *Templates are stored sets of formatting and text that may be used to create specialized word processing documents, spreadsheets, and databases.*

Autostart Templates

- IN OPENING WORKS DIALOG BOX -

1. Click **Use a Template**... `T`

   OR

   a. Click **File** menu .... `Alt` + `F`

   b. Click **Templates** .... `T`

2. Click **Choose a Template Group**.................. `Alt` + `C`

3. Select group .... `PgDn` , `F4`

4. Click in **Choose a Template Category** .... `Alt` + `H`

5. Select desired category... `PgDn`

6. Click **Choose a Template** .... `Alt` + `S`

7. Select desired template... `PgDn`

8. Click **OK**....................... .... `Enter`

Create Custom Template

Saves formatting, text and other features to use when creating new files.

1. Create a new word processing document, spreadsheet or database.

   OR

   Open desired existing file.

(continued...)

CREATE CUSTOM TEMPLATE (continued)

2. Add any text, graphics, settings or formatting you wish to include in template.

3. Click **File** menu... `Alt` + `F`

4. Click **Save As** .... `A`

5. Click **Template** .... `Alt` + `P`

6. Type template name..*name*

7. Click **OK**.. `Enter`

> *NOTE:* *If a template has been previously defined, Works will ask permission to overwrite the original template file.*

Rename Template

1. Click **File** menu... `Alt` + `F`

2. Click **Templates** .... `T`

3. Click **Choose a Template Group**...................... `Alt` + `C`

4. Select desired group............................... `PgDn` + `F4`

5. Click in **Choose a Template Category** .... `Alt` + `H`

6. Select desired category....................................... `PgDn`

7. Click **Choose a Template** .... `Alt` + `S`

8. Select desired template.. `PgDn`

9. Click **Rename** .... `Alt` + `R`

10. Type new name..*name* in **Name** text box.

(continued...)

RENAME TEMPLATE (continued)

11. Click **R**ename .... Alt + R

12. Click **C**lose.............................. Alt + C , Enter

13. Click **OK**... Enter

Delete Template

1. Click **F**ile menu.............................. Alt + F

2. Click **T**emplates .... T

3. Click **C**hoose a Template Group.................. Alt + C

4. Select desired group .... PgDn , F4

5. Click C**h**oose a Template Category............... Alt + H

6. Select desired category............................... PgDn

7. Click Choo**s**e a Template .... Alt + S

8. Select desired template................................ PgDn

9. Click **D**elete .... D

10. Click **Y**es .... Enter

COPY OR MOVE TEXT, CHARTS, CELLS OR ENTRIES BETWEEN WORKS TOOLS

1. View file with information to copy or move.

2. Select area you wish to copy or move.

(continued...)

12

COPY OR MOVE TEXT, CHARTS, CELLS OR ENTRIES BETWEEN WORKS TOOLS (continued)

3. Click **E**dit menu.................................... `Alt` + `E`

   To copy:

   Choose **C**opy .... `C`

   To move:

   Choose **Cu**t .... `T`

4. View file to receive information.

5. Place insertion point at desired location.

6. Click **E**dit menu.................................... `Alt` + `E`

7. Click **P**aste .... `P`

FORMAT PAGES

Set Margins

1. Click **F**ile menu.................................... `Alt` + `F`

2. Click **Pa**ge Setup.. `G`

3. Click **M**argins tab.................................... `Alt` + `M`

4. Click desired option from the following:

   • **T**op Margin .... `Alt` + `T`

   • **B**ottom Margin .... `Alt` + `B`

   • **L**eft Margin .... `Alt` + `L`

   • **R**ight Margin .... `Alt` + `R`

   • He**a**der Margin .... `Alt` + `A`

   • **F**ooter Margin .... `Alt` + `F`

(continued...)

SET MARGINS (continued)

4. Type measurement...*number*

5. Repeat steps 4 and 5 as necessary.

6. Click **OK**.. Enter

Set Page Size

1. Click **File** menu .... Alt

2. Click **Page Setup**.. G

3. Click **Source, Size and Orientation** tab .... Alt + S

4. To change to another pre-selected paper size:

    a. Click Paper size... Alt + I

    b. Select desired size .... ↓ , F4

    ### If custom size was selected, choose desired option from the following:

    *   Width... Alt + W

    *   Height.. Alt + G

5. Type measurement for new page size ....*number*

6. Click **OK**.. Enter

Set Page Orientation

1. Click **File** menu... Alt + F

2. Click **Page Setup**.. G

(continued...)

14

SET PAGE ORIENTATION (continued)

3. Choose desired orientation from the following:

    *   Portrait .... `Alt` + `P`

    *   Landscape .... `Alt` + `L`

4. Click **OK** .... `Enter`

Number Pages

> *NOTE: Page numbers only appear in the document
> window in Page Layout view (see page 27).*

1. Click **View** menu .... `Alt` + `Y`

2. Click **Headers** and Footers .... `H`

3. Choose desired page number location:

    *   Header .... `Alt` + `E`
        to position number at top center of page.

    *   Footer .... `Alt` + `F`
        to position number at bottom
        center of page.

4. Type code .... *code*
    to align numbering, if desired
    (centered numbers are preset)

    *   Type .... `&` + `I`
        for left-alignment

    *   Type .... `&` + `R`
        for right-alignment.

5. Type code for page number .... `&` + `P`

6. Click **OK** .... `Enter`

Suppress Page Number on First Page

1. Click **V**iew menu .... Alt + V

2. Click **H**eaders and Footers .... H

3. Click desired option from the following:

   • **N**o header on 1st page .... Alt + N

   • N**o** footer on 1st page .... Alt + O

4. Click **OK** .... Enter

Change Starting Page Number

1. Place insertion point where you would like new page numbering to begin.

2. Click **F**ile menu .... Alt + F

3. Click **Page Setup** .... G

4. Click **O**ther Options tab .... O

5. Click **1**st page number: .... Alt + 1

6. Type new page number ....*number* in text box.

7. Click **OK** .... Enter

Turn Off Page Numbering

1. Place insertion point where you would like page numbering to end.

2. Click **V**iew menu .... Alt + V

3. Click **H**eaders and Footers .... H

4. Select page number code (&p) from Header or Footer text box.

(continued...)

16

5. Press .... `Del`

6. Click **OK** .... `Enter`

CREATE HEADERS AND FOOTERS

Headers and footers print at the top or bottom of every page and can contain titles, page numbers, dates and other text. Headers and footers may contain only one line of text or codes (for multi-line headers and footers in the word processor, see page 55). Check Print Preview (page 20) or Page Layout view (page 27) to see how headers and footers will appear on the printed page.

1. Click **View** menu .... `Alt` + `V`

2. Click **Headers and Footers** .... `H`

3. Click **Header** .... `Alt` + `E`

   OR

   Click **Footer** .... `Alt` + `F`

4. Type desired combination of text or codes for header or footer.

   • Type .... `&` `L`
     to left-align following text

   • Type .... `&` `R`
     to right-align following text.

   • Type .... `&` `c`
     to center following text.

   • Type .... `&` `P`
     to print page number.

(continued...)

CREATE HEADERS AND FOOTERS (continued)

- Type .... `&` `F`
  to print filename.

- Type .... `&` `D`
  to print date.

- Type .... `&` `N`
  to print long format date.

- Type .... `&` `T`
  to print time.

- Type .... `&` `&`
  to print an ampersand (&).

  NOTE: *Separate any combination of page number, date,*
  filename, time and ampersand codes from each
  other by at least one space.

5. Click **OK**... `Enter`

Set Header and Footer Margins

1. Click **File** menu............................... `Alt` + `F`

2. Click **Page Setup**................................... `G`

3. Click **Margin** tab .... `Alt` + `M`

4. Click **Header Margin** .... `Alt` + `A`

   OR

   Click **Footer Margin** .... `Alt` + `F`

5. Type new margin measurements.............................*numbers*

   NOTE: *Distance is from top or bottom of page, not*
   distance from page text.

6. Click **OK**... `Enter`

Suppress Header or Footer (First Page)

1. Click **View** menu.. `Alt` + `V`

2. Click **Headers and Footers** .... `H`

3. Click **No header on 1st page**....................... `Alt` + `N`

   OR

   Click **No footer on 1st page** .... `Alt` + `O`

Delete Headers and Footers

1. Click **View** menu.. `Alt` + `V`

2. Click **Headers and Footers** .... `H`

3. Click **Header** .... `Alt` + `E`

   OR

   Click **Footer**.. `Alt` + `F`

4. Select all text.

5. Press .... `Del`

6. Click **OK**.. `Enter`

PRINT

Printer Setup

1. Click **File** menu.. `Alt` + `F`

2. Click **Printer Setup** .... `R`

3. Select printer from **Printer** text box... `Alt` + `P` , `F4`

   To access additional settings:

4. Choose **Setup** .... `Alt` + `S`

(continued...)

PRINTER SETUP (continued)

5. Make desired setup changes (dialog box will be different for each printer).

6. Click **OK**.. `Enter`
    to exit setup dialog, if necessary.

7. Click **OK**.. `Enter`

Print File

– ON TOOLBAR –

1. Click **Print button** .... 🖨️

    OR

    a. Click **File** menu .... `Alt` + `F`

    b. Click **Print** .... `P`

    c. Click **Number of Copies** .... `Alt` + `C`

    d. Type desired number of copies..............................*number*

3. To limit pages of files to print:

    a. Click **Pages**.. `Alt` + `P`

    b. Click **From**.. `Alt` + `F`

    c. Type first page to print ....*number*

    d. Click **To** .... `Alt` + `T`

    e. Type last page to print..............................*number*

4. Click **Draft Quality Printing** .... `Alt` + `D`
    to select fast printing ⊠ , if desired.

5. Click **OK**.. `Enter`

20

Cancel Printing

– IN PRINT DIALOG BOX –

Click **Cancel** .... `Esc`

Preview File

Shows how a document, spreadsheet or database will appear on the printed page. Many formatting features, such as page numbering and headers and footers, appear only in print preview and in print.

- ON TOOLBAR -

Click... `🔍`

OR

a.   Click **File** menu... `Alt` + `F`

b.   Click **Print Preview** .... `V`

To view previous page:

Click **Previous** .... `Alt` + `R`

OR

Press .... `PgUp`

To view next page:

Click **Next** .... `Alt` + `N`

OR

Press .... `PgDn`

To enlarge page:

a.   Place pointer on desired area.

b.   Click **Zoom In**... `Alt` + `I`

OR

Click page.   (continued...)

PREVIEW FILE (continued)

To reduce page:

Click **Zoom Out**..[E] + [O]

To print document::

Click **Print**..[Alt] + [P]

To return to document pane:

Click **Cancel** ....[Esc]

GET HELP

The Works Help feature is like a manual on a disk. It may be accessed in several ways.

How to Use Help

1. Click **Help** menu....................................[Alt] + [H]

2. Click **How to use help** ....[H]

3. Follow instructions on screen.

General Help

1. Click **Help** menu ....[Alt] + [H]

    *NOTE: Choice displayed will depend on which Works tool
    is in use.*

2. Click displayed choice:

    • **Word Processor Overview** ....[W]

    • **Spreadsheet Overview**....................................[S]

    • **Charting Overview** ....[C]

(continued...)

GENERAL HELP (continued)

- Communications Overview .... O
- Form View .... F
- List View L
- Query View .... Q
- Report View .... R

3. Follow instructions on screen.

Basic Help

1. Click Help menu .... Alt + H
2. Click Basic Skills .... B
3. Follow instructions on screen.

Context-Sensitive Help

1. Select or view desired topic.
2. Press F1

CHECK SPELLING

Scans for incorrect spelling, capitalization and hyphenation.

1. Place insertion point where you would like
   spelling check to begin.

2. Click **Check Spelling** button .... ✓

   OR

   a. Click **Tools** menu .... Alt + O

(continued...)

CHECK SPELLING (continued)

    b. Click **Spelling** .... `S`

Words not in the Works dictionary are displayed for correction.

3.   Select desired option:

- Ignore.. `Alt` + `I`
  to resume scanning.

- Ignore All.. `Alt` + `G`
  to resume scanning and pass over
  future occurrences of the word.

- Add.. `Alt` + `A`
  to add word to dictionary for future checks.

- Change To.. `Alt` + `T`
  to type correction in text box.

- Suggest .... `Alt` + `S`
  to select from **Suggestions** text box.

- Change.. `Alt` + `C`
  to correct word in document.

- Change All....................................... `Alt` + `E`
  to correct all matching words in document.

4.   Click **OK** when spell check is complete.................. `Enter`
when spell check is complete.

Ignore Proper Nouns

– IN THE SPELLING DIALOG BOX –

Click **Skip capitalized words** .... `Alt` + `K`

Set Speller to Make Suggestions

– IN SPELLING DIALOG BOX –

Click **A**lways **S**uggest..................................... `Alt` + `L`

SET FILES TO OPEN WHEN WORKS IS STARTED

Opens specified documents automatically every time you start Works.

1. Open files you would like to open when Works is started.

2. Arrange windows as desired.

3. Click **F**ile menu.. `Alt` + `F`

4. Click **S**ave **W**orkspace .... `W`

REMOVE FILES SET TO OPEN WHEN WORKS IS STARTED

1. Click **T**ools menu.. `Alt` + `O`

2. Click **O**ptions.. `O`

3. Click **U**se Saved Workspace.............. `Alt` + `U`
   to clear ☐.

4. Click **OK**.. `Enter`

DIAL TELEPHONE NUMBER

NOTE: *If computer has a modem, telephone numbers may be dialed automatically from any Works files, but not from a blank workspace. See page 246 to set modem settings.*

1. Select number in document to dial.

(continued...)

DIAL TELEPHONE NUMBER (continued)

2. Click **Tools** menu.. `Alt` + `O`

3. Click **Dial this Number**... `D`

4. Click **OK**... `Enter`
    after connection.

    OR

    Click **Cancel**.. `Esc`

SHARE INFORMATION WITH OTHER APPLICATIONS

*Works can access files created by other applications in two ways: by **translation** (Works translates special codes from the file into codes that it recognizes), or as **text** (text files don't have special characters that need to be translated). Works can open files created in Microsoft Word, Microsoft Word for Windows, Microsoft Windows Write, WordPerfect, Lotus 1-2-3 and dBase, among others. If the desired application type doesn't appear in the File Type list, save and retrieve the file as text.*

Translate File Created by Another Application

1. Click **File** menu...................................... `Alt` + `F`

2. Click **Open Existing File**.................................... `O`

    NOTE: If necessary, change to drive or subdirectory containing desired file.

3. Click **List Files of Type**............................. `Alt` + `T`

4. Choose desired file type............................... `↓`

    NOTE: If file type is not listed, choose text file.

(continued...)

TRANSLATE FILE CREATED BY ANOTHER APPLICATION (continued)

5. Click **File Name** .... Alt + N

6. Choose desired file .... ↓

7. Click **OK**. .... Enter

Save Document in Another Format

1. View document you wish to save.

2. Click **File** menu .... Alt + F

3. Click **Save As** .... A

4. Type name of file to save .... *name*

5. Click **Save File as Type** .... Alt + T

6. Select desired file type .... ↓

7. Click **OK** .... Enter

Word Processor

THE WORD PROCESSOR WINDOW

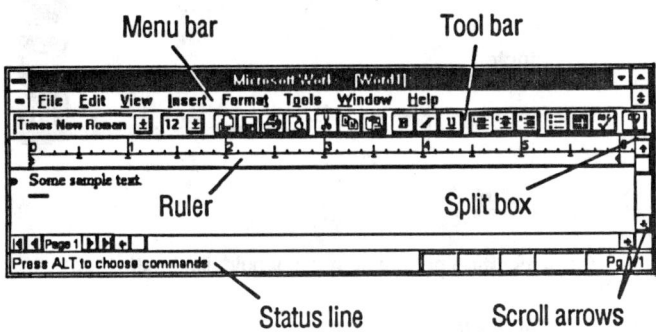

Menu bar   Tool bar

Ruler   Split box

Status line   Scroll arrows

CHANGE WINDOW APPEARANCE

1. Click <u>V</u>iew menu.. **Alt** + **V**

2. Choose desired options to select (✓) or deselect:

   • Tool<u>b</u>ar.. **B**

   • <u>Z</u>oom .... **Z**
     to enlarge or reduce screen display.

   • <u>N</u>ormal.. **N**
     to restore from Page Layout and Draft View.

   • Pa<u>g</u>e Layout.. **G**

   • Dr<u>a</u>ft View... **A**
     to put all lettering in same font and size.

   • Wra<u>p</u> for Window... **P**
     to fit text on screen.

(continued...)

CHANGE WINDOW APPEARANCE (continued)

- All Characters .... **L**
  to view special characters and codes.

- Ruler .... **R**

- Footnotes... **F**

- Headers and Footers .... **H**

ADD TEXT

1. Place insertion point where you would like to add text.

2. Click mouse button.

3. Type new text..*text*

EDIT TEXT

Tell Works to Replace Selected Text

1. Click Tools menu... **Alt** + **O**

2. Click Options.. **O**

3. Click Typing Replaces Selection .... **Y**
   to select (☒).

Replace Selected Text

1. Select Typing Replaces Selection (see above).

2. Select text to replace.

3. Type new text.

Overtype Existing Text

1. Place insertion point where new text is to be typed.

2. Press .... Ins

   OR

   a. Click **Tools** menu .... Alt + O

   b. Click **Options** .... O

   c. Click **Overtype** V

   NOTE: *An alert (OVR) will appear on the status line while*
   overtype is selected.

3. Type text..*text*

Delete Single Character

1. Place cursor next to character you wish to delete.

2. Press .... Backspace
   to delete character to the left.

   OR

   Press .... Del
   to delete character to the right.

Delete Selected Text or Object

1. Select text or object you wish to delete.

2. Press .... Backspace or Del

   OR

   a. Click **Edit** menu .... Alt + E

   b. Click **Clear** .... E

Move Text or Objects

Text or objects may be moved by the drag and drop method from one place to another in a document, or from one file to another. If information is moved from another application to the word processing document, it might automatically be embedded (see page 78).

If moving information from one file to another:

1. Arrange screen to view both windows.

2. Select text or object to move.

3. With insertion point on selection, press and hold mouse button and drag to new location.

   NOTE: *Insertion point will change appearance to indicate selection is being dragged. If insertion point changes to a circle with a slash, it indicates that the selection cannot be moved to that location with this method.*

4. Release mouse button.

Copy Text to Clipboard

1. Select text you wish to copy.

2. Click .... 📑

   OR

   a. Click **E**dit menu .... `Alt` + `E`

   b. Click **C**opy .... `C`

   OR

   Press .... `Ctrl` + `C`

Cut Text to Clipboard

1. Select text you wish to copy.

2. Click .... `✂`

    a. Click **E**dit menu .... `Alt` + `E`

    b. Click **Cut** .... `T`

    OR

    Press .... `Ctrl` + `X`

Paste Text from Clipboard

1. Place insertion point where you would like to paste.

2. Click .... `📋`

    OR

    a. Click **E**dit menu .... `Alt` + `E`

    b. Click **P**aste .... `P`

    OR

    Press .... `Ctrl` + `V`

MOVE AROUND IN WORD PROCESSOR DOCUMENT

Scroll Through Document

Scroll to view different parts of a document too large to fit in the window. Scrolling does not move the insertion point, however.

(continued...)

SCROLL THROUGH DOCUMENT (continued)

Click scroll bar arrows.. ⬆ ⬇
until desired screen appears.

OR

Click and drag scroll bar button until desired screen appears.

OR

Click scroll bar until desired screen appears.

Move Insertion Point Using Keyboard

One character left.. ←

One character right .... →

One line up .... ↑

One line down .... ↓

One word left.. Ctrl + ←

One word right .... Ctrl + →

One paragraph up.. Ctrl + ↑

One paragraph down.. Ctrl + ↓

Beginning of line.. Home

End of line.. End

Beginning of document.............................. Ctrl + Home

(continued...)

MOVE INSERTION POINT USING KEYBOARD (continued)

End of document...	Ctrl + End
One window up..	PgUp
One window down..	PgDn
Beginning of window	Ctrl + PgUp
End of window	Ctrl + PgDn
To move between panes of a split window........................	F6

SELECT OR HIGHLIGHT TO EDIT

Select Any Amount of Text

Click and drag over text or objects you wish to select.

OR

Press .... Shift + ← , →

Select One Word

Double-click the word.

OR

a. Place insertion point on word.

b. Press F8

Select One Line

Click margin to left of desired line.

OR

a. Place insertion point at beginning of line.

b. Press.. **Shift** + **End**

Select One Sentence

Click and drag over sentence.

OR

a. Place insertion point in sentence.

b. Press **F8**
    three times.

Select Multiple Lines

Click and drag margin to left of desired lines.

OR

Press .... **Shift** + **↓**

OR

Press .... **Shift** + **↑**

Select One Paragraph

Double-click in margin to left of paragraph.

OR

a. Place insertion point in paragraph

b. Press **F8**
    four times.

Select Entire Document

1. Hold... `Ctrl`

2. Click in left margin.

3. Release.. `Ctrl`

OR

Press.. `F8`
five times.

TOOLBAR

> *NOTE: Click toolbar buttons to activate. See page 8 to
> view, hide or add buttons to toolbar.*

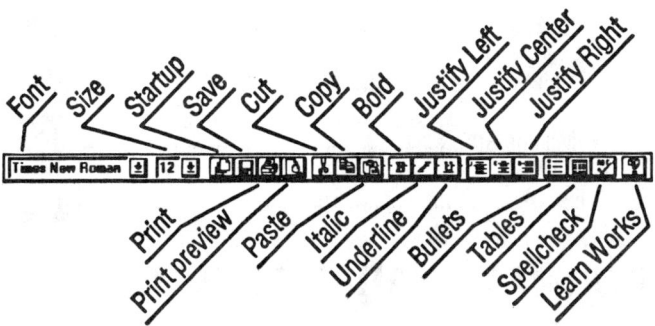

RULER

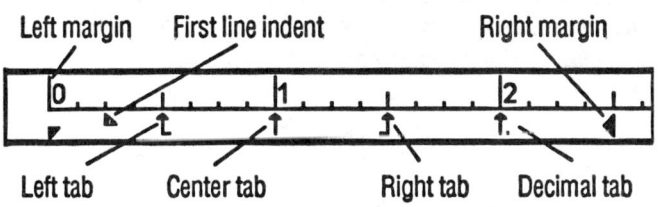

(continued...)

View or Hide Ruler

1. Click **V**iew menu... Alt + V

2. Click **R**uler... R
   to select ☒ or deselect.

Change Ruler Measurement Units

1. Click **T**ools menu... Alt + O

2. Click **O**ptions.. O

3. Click desired unit (to select ◉) of measure from the following:

   • **I**nches... I

   • **C**entimeters .... E

   • **P**ica... P

   • Poin**t**s .... T

   • Millimete**r**s.. R

4. Click **OK**.. ↵

FORMAT CHARACTERS

Set Character Styles

*Includes font, text characteristics, and size, and can be chosen before typing text or for selected text. Multiple styles may be set at once from the **Font & Style** dialog box, or styles may be selected individually using the Toolbar or shortcut keystrokes.*

(continued...)

Underline

1. Select text to be underlined.

    OR

    Place insertion point where you will type new, underlined text.

2. Click.. $\boxed{\underline{\text{U}}}$

    OR

    Press.. $\boxed{\textbf{Ctrl}}$ + $\boxed{\text{U}}$

Bold

1. Select text to be bold faced.

    OR

    Place insertion point where you will type new, bold faced text.

2. Click .... $\boxed{\textbf{B}}$

    OR

    Press.. $\boxed{\textbf{Ctrl}}$ + $\boxed{\textbf{B}}$

Italics

1. Select text to be italicized.

    OR

    Place insertion point where you will type new, italicized text.

(continued...)

38

ITALICS (continued)

2. Click .... $\boxed{I}$

    OR

    Press.. $\boxed{\text{Ctrl}}$ + $\boxed{\text{I}}$

Subscript

1. Select text to be subscripted.

    OR

    Place insertion point where you will type new, subscripted text.

2. Press.. $\boxed{\text{Ctrl}}$ + $\boxed{=}$

Superscript

1. Select text to be superscripted.

    OR

    Place insertion point where you will type new, superscripted text.

2. Press............................. $\boxed{\text{Ctrl}}$ + $\boxed{\text{Shift}}$ + $\boxed{+}$

Strikethrough

1. Select text you would like to strike through.

    OR

    Place insertion point where you will type new, strikethrough text.

(continued...)

STRIKETHROUGH (continued)

2. Click **Format** menu .... `Alt` + `T`

3. Click **Font and Style** .... `T`

4. Click **Strikethrough** to select (⊠) .... `Alt` + `T`

5. Click **OK** .... `↵`

Color

1. Select text to be colored.

   OR

   Place insertion point where you will type new, colored text.

2. Click **Format** menu .... `Alt` + `T`

3. Click **Font and Style** .... `F`

4. Click **Color** list box... `Alt` + `O`

5. Choose desired color from color list.............................. `↓`

6. Click **OK** .... `↵`

Remove Single Style

1. Select text to be styled.

   OR

   Place insertion point where you will type new text.

2. Click desired button or press shortcut keys for style you wish to remove.

40

Remove All Styles

1. Select text whose styles are to be removed.

    OR

    Place insertion point where you will type new, plain text.

2. Press..

Select Font

1. Select text whose font you wish to change.

    OR

    Place insertion point where you will type new text in a different font.

2. Click **Font** drop down button...📥

3. Select desired font...⬆ ⬇

Select Font Size

1. Select text whose font size you wish to change.

    OR

    Place insertion point where you will type new text in a different font size.

2. Click **Size** drop-down button ....📥

3. Select desired size...⬆ , ⬇

Select Multiple Character Styles at Once

> *NOTE: Opening the **Font & Style** dialog box is also a way to
> set font and font size using the keyboard.*

1. Select text to be formatted.

    OR

    Place insertion point where you will type new, formatted text.

2. Click **Format** menu .... `Alt` + `T`

3. Click **Font & Style** .... `F`

4. Select desired font .... `↑` , `↓`

5. Choose desired **Styles** to select (⊠) or deselect
    (☐) from the following:

    • Bold.. `Alt` + `B`

    • Italic .... `Alt` + `I`

    • Underline.. `Alt` + `U`

    • Strikethrough .... `Alt` + `T`

6. Select desired size. .... `Alt` + `S` , `↑` , `↓`

7. Choose a Position to select (◉) from the following:

    • Normal .... `Alt` + `N`

    • Superscript .... `Alt` + `P`

    • Subscript... `Alt` + `C`

8. Select desired color.............................. `Alt` + `O` , `↓`

9. Click **OK**.. `↵`

FORMAT TEXT

Format Paragraphs

> *NOTE:* *A paragraph is ended by a hard return (Enter)*
> *Paragraphs and other text can be formatted before*
> *being typed or after being typed by selecting the*
> *text, then formatting it.*

Indent First Line of Paragraph

Press .... Tab

Align Text

> *NOTE:* *Unless otherwise specified, text in Works will be*
> *left aligned. Text may also be right-aligned,*
> *centered, or fully justified by using the **Indents &***
> ***Spacing** dialog box, the Toolbar or shortcut*
> *keystrokes.*

Right-Align Text

1. Select text to be right-aligned.

   OR

   Place insertion point where you will type new right
   aligned text.

2. Click ....

   OR

   Press .... Ctrl + R

Center Text

1. Select text to be center aligned.

    OR

    Place insertion point where you will type new centered aligned text.

2. Click .... `⫤`
    OR

    Press... `Ctrl` + `E`

Left-Align Text

1. Select text to be left-aligned.

    OR

    Place insertion point where you will type new left aligned text.

2. Click .... `⫤`

    OR

    Press... `Ctrl` + `L`

Justify Text

1. Select text to be justified.

    OR

    Place insertion point where you will type new justified text.

2. Click .... `⫤`

    OR

    Press... `Ctrl` + `J`

Set Line Spacing

1. Select text to be respaced.

   OR

   Place insertion point where you will type new text with different line spacing.

2. Choose one of the following line spacing options:

   - Single space.................................... `Ctrl` + `1`

   - Double space .... `Ctrl` + `2`

   - One and one-half space .... `Ctrl` + `5`

Set Precise Line Spacing

1. Click **Format** menu .... `Alt` + `T`

2. Click **Paragraph** .... `A`

3. Click **Breaks and Spacing** tab .... `Alt` + `S`

4. Click **Between Lines** text box .... `Alt` + `L`

5. Type desired line spacing
   as a decimal number.................................*number*

6. Click **OK**.. `↵`

Set First Line Indent

1. Click **Format** menu .... `Alt` + `T`

2. Click **Paragraph** .... `A`

3. Click **Quick Formats** tab .... `Alt` + `Q`

4. Click **1st line indent** .... `Alt` + `1`

*An example of formatted text will appear in the **Sample** area.*

5. Click **OK**.. `↵`

Set Bulleted Paragraphs

1. Select paragraphs to bullet.

   OR

   Place insertion point where bullets are to begin.

2. Click **Bullet** button .... 〔▤〕

Undo Bullets

1. Select paragraphs whose bullets you wish to remove.

2. Click **Forma_t** menu .... 〔Alt〕 + 〔T〕

3. Click **P_aragraph** .... 〔A〕

3. Click **_Quick Formats** tab .... 〔Alt〕 + 〔Q〕

5. Click **_Normal** .... 〔Alt〕 + 〔N〕

6. Click **OK** .... 〔⏎〕

Set Double Indents

1. Select paragraph to indent.

2. Click **Forma_t** menu .... 〔Alt〕 + 〔T〕

3. Click **P_aragraph** .... 〔A〕

4. Click **_Quick Formats** tab .... 〔Alt〕 + 〔Q〕

5. Click **Quo_tation** .... 〔Alt〕 + 〔T〕

*An example of formatted text will appear in the **Sample** area.*

6. Click **OK** .... 〔⏎〕

Set a Nested Double Indent

> *NOTE:* *Indented text will be aligned indented left and right margins.*

1. Select paragraph to indent.

2. Press.. **Ctrl** + **N**

3. Repeat for each level of indent.

Undo Nested Indent

1. Select paragraph whose indents you wish to remove.

2. Press.. **Ctrl** + **M**

3. Repeat for each level of indent.

Set a Hanging Indent

> *NOTE:* *The first line of a paragraph set with a hanging indent will be flush left; the rest of the lines will be indented one tab stop.*

1. Select paragraph to indent.

2. Press.. **Ctrl** + **H**

Undo Hanging Indent

1. Select paragraph whose hanging indent you wish to remove.

2. Press.. **Ctrl** + **G**

Set Custom Indent

1. Select paragraph to indent.

2. Click **Format** menu .... **Alt** + **T**

(continued...)

SET CUSTOM INDENT (continued)

3. Click **Paragraph** .... `A`

4. Click **Indents and Alignment** tab .... `I`

5. Choose desired indent to change:

    - Left indent: .... `Alt` + `E`

    - Right indent: .... `Alt` + `G`

    - First line indent: .... `Alt` + `F`
      to display a negative number
      for hanging indent.

5. Type desired indent in text box ....*number*

6. Click **OK** .... `↵`

Set Paragraph Indents, Spacing, Breaks and Alignment Manually

> *NOTE:*   *Use the Paragraph dialog box to access paragraph format options not available from the Toolbar, and to set several paragraph format characteristics at once. The Sample area of the dialog box shows the result of the currently selected options.*

1. Select paragraphs to format.

    OR

    Place insertion point where formatted paragraphs are to begin.

2. Click **Format** menu .... `Alt` + `T`

3. Click **Paragraph** .... `A`

(continued...)

48

SET PARAGRAPH INDENTS, SPACING, BREAKS AND ALIGNMENT MANUALLY (continued)

4. Click **Indents and Alignment** tab .... `Alt` + `I`
   if desired.

5. Click desired indent to change:

   • Left indent: .... `Alt` + `E`

   • Right indent: .... `Alt` + `G`

   • First line indent: .... `Alt` + `F`
     to display a negative number
     for hanging indent.

6. Type desired indent in text box .... *number*

7. Choose desired **Alignment** from the following:

   • Left .... `Alt` + `L`

   • Right .... `Alt` + `R`

   • Center .... `Alt` + `C`

   • Justify .... `Alt` + `J`

8. Click **Bulleted** .... `Alt` + `B`
   to create bulleted paragraphs, if desired.

9. Click **Breaks and Spacing,** if desired .... `Alt` + `S`

10. Click desired **Line Spacing** option from the following:

   • Between Lines: .... `Alt` + `I`

   • Before paragraph: .... `Alt` + `E`

   • After paragraph: .... `Alt` + `A`

(continued...)

SET PARAGRAPH INDENTS, SPACING, BREAKS AND ALIGNMENT MANUALLY (continued)

11. Type desired new line spacing number ....*number*

12. Choose desired **Paragraph Breaks** option
    to select (☒) or deselect (☐) from the following:

    • Don't break paragraph .... `Alt` + `K`

    • Keep paragraph with next.......................... `Alt` + `W`

13. Click **OK**... `⏎`

FORMAT PAGES

Insert Page Break

Starts a new page before the previous page.

1. Place insertion point where new page will begin.

2. Press... `Ctrl` + `⏎`

   OR

   a. Click **Insert** menu.............................. `Alt` + `I`

   b. Click **Page Break**.. `B`

Remove Page Break

1. Place insertion point at beginning of line containing break.

2. Press .... `Del`

Keep Paragraph from Breaking Over Two Pages

1. Select paragraph.

(continued...)

KEEP PARAGRAPH FROM BREAKING OVER TWO PAGES (continued)

2. Click **Forma̱t** menu .... `Alt` + `T`
3. Click **P̱aragraph** .... `A`
4. Click **Breaks and S̱pacing** .... `Alt` + `S`
5. Click **Don't brea̱k paragraph** .... `Alt` + `K`
   to select (☒).
6. Click **OK** .... `←`

Keep Two Paragraphs Together on Same Page

1. Select first paragraph.
2. Click **Forma̱t** menu .... `Alt` + `T`
3. Click **P̱aragraph** .... `A`
4. Click **Breaks and S̱pacing** .... `Alt` + `S`
5. Click **Keep paragraph w̱ith next** .... `Alt` + `W`
   to select (☒).
6. Click **OK** .... `←`

Repaginate Document

> *NOTE:* *The status bar at the bottom of the window tells the total number of pages in a document and the current page number.*

1. Click **Ṯools** menu .... `Alt` + `O`
2. Click **Paginate Ṉow** .... `N`

SET TAB STOPS

NOTE: Works has preset tab stops every .5 of an inch.

Change Preset Tab Stops

1. Select paragraph(s) containing tab stops to change.

    OR

    Place insertion point at beginning of new
    paragraph to set tabs for subsequent text.

2. Click **Format** menu .... `Alt` + `T`

3. Click **Tabs** .... `T`

4. Click **Position** .... `Alt` + `P`

5. Type starting position...*number*
    for new tab spacing measurement.

6. Click **Default Tab Spacing:** .... `Alt` + `S`

7. Type measurement...*number*

    *NOTE: Type measurements in inches ("), centimeters
    (cm), picas (pi) or points (pt).*

8. Click **Insert**... `Alt` + `I`

9. Click **OK**.. `↵`

Set Custom Tab Stops Using Ruler

1. Select paragraph(s) containing tab stops to change.

    OR

    Place insertion point at beginning of new
    paragraph to set tabs for subsequent text.

(continued...)

SET CUSTOM TAB STOPS USING RULER (continued)

2.   View ruler (see page 36.)

   *NOTE: Preset tabs will appear just below ruler
            measurement markings.*

3.   Position pointer just beneath desired
     tab measurement marking and double-click.

   OR

   For left tab:

   a. Position pointer just beneath desired
      tab measurement marking.

   b. Click once.

4.   Choose desired tab alignment from the following options:

   • Left...| Alt | + | L |

   • Center..| Alt | + | E |

   • Right ....| Alt | + | R |

   • Decimal ....| Alt | + | D |

5.   Choose desired leader from the following:

   • None...| Alt | + | N |

   • 1..... ....| Alt | + | 1 |

   • 2—   ....| Alt | + | 2 |

   • 3___   ....| Alt | + | 3 |

   • 4═══ ....| Alt | + | 4 |

(continued...)

SET CUSTOM TAB STOPS USING RULER (continued)

6. Click **Insert**.. **Alt** + **I**

7. Click **OK**... **↵**

Set Custom Tab Stops in Tabs Dialog Box

1. Select paragraph(s) containing tab stops to change.

   OR

   Place insertion point at beginning of
   new paragraph to set tabs for subsequent text.

2. Click **Format** menu .... **Alt** + **T**

3. Click **Tabs**... **T**

4. Click **Position:** .... **Alt** + **P**

5. Type desired tab location ....*number*

   *NOTE: Type measurements in inches ("), centimeters
             (cm), picas (pi) or points (pt).*

6. Choose desired tab alignment from the following options:

   • **Left**... **Alt** + **L**

   • **Center**... **Alt** + **E**

   • **Right** .... **Alt** + **R**

   • **Decimal** .... **Alt** + **D**

(continued...)

SET CUSTOM TAB STOPS IN TABS DIALOG BOX (continued)

7. Click desired leader to select (⊙):

- <u>N</u>one... `Alt` + `N`
- <u>1</u>.......... .... `Alt` + `1`
- <u>2</u>— .... `Alt` + `2`
- <u>3</u> .... `Alt` + `3`
- <u>4</u>— .... `Alt` + `4`

8. Click <u>I</u>nsert... `Alt` + `I`

9. Repeat steps 4 to 8 to set additional tabs.

10. Click **OK**.. `↵`

Remove Tab Stop

1. Select paragraph(s) containing tab stops to change.

   OR

   Place insertion point at beginning of
   new paragraph to set tabs for subsequent text.

2. View ruler (see page 36).

3. Click and drag tab stop off ruler.

LISTS

Create List

1. Set tab stop for each column in list.

   NOTE: *Use decimal-aligned or right-aligned tab stops for*
   columns of numbers.

(continued...)

CREATE LIST (continued)

2. Type text, pressing **Tab** between columns .... `Tab`

3. Press.. `Shift` + `↵`
   at end of each line.

   *(Pressing Shift+Enter allows formatting of list
   as a single paragraph.)*

Add Column to List

1. Select entire list.

2. Add desired type of tab stop at new column location.

   *(See **Set Tabs**, page 5.)*

3. Change position of remaining tab stops.

Position insertion point at new tab stop

4. Press .... `Tab`

5. Type text ....*text*
   for new column.

Create a Multi-Line Header or Footer

NOTE: *Paragraph headers and footers can include a
drawing or other object. Text in header and footer
paragraphs may be formatted in the same way as
other document text. Header or footer margins
may need to be increased for multi-line headers or
footers (see below). Check Print Preview or Page
Layout View to see how headers and footers will
appear on the printed page.*

1. Click **View** menu .... `Alt` + `V`

(continued...)

CREATE A MULTI-LINE HEADER OR FOOTER (continued)

2. Click **H**eaders and Footers...................................... `H`

3. Click **U**se header and footer paragraphs......... `Alt` + `U`

4. Click **OK** .... `←`

5. Type text to include in header to right
    of letter H at top of page 1.

    To start new line:

    Type... `Shift` + `←`

    NOTE: For no header, do not type text.

6. Type text to include in footer to right of
    letter F at top of page 1.

    To start a new line:

    Type... `Shift` + `←`

    *NOTES: The page place holder may be deleted or selected
    and moved to the header.*

    *For no footer, delete or move page place holder
    and do not type text.*

Turn off Paragraph Headers and Footers

1. Click **V**iew menu .... `Alt` + `V`

2. Click **H**eaders and Footers...................................... `H`

3. Click **U**se header and footer paragraphs......... `Alt` + `U`
    to clear.

4. Click **OK** .... `←`

THESAURUS

Displays synonyms of words.

1. Select word to look up.

2. Click **T**ools menu .... `Alt` + `O`

3. Click **T**hesaurus .... `T`

4. Select **M**eanings list box .... `Alt` + `M`

5. Select correct meaning.

6. Select S**y**nonyms list box .... `Alt` + `Y`

7. Select best word.

8. Click **C**hange .... `Alt` + `C`

   OR

   Click **Cancel** .... `Esc`

COUNT WORDS

1. Select text to count.

   *NOTE: To count entire document, there is no need to
             select text.*

2. Click **T**ools menu .... `Alt` + `O`

3. Click **Word C**ount .... `C`

4. Click **OK** .... `⏎`
   to close word count dialog box
   and return to document.

HYPHENATE WORDS

NOTE: *When Works is set to automatically hyphenate words, it inserts what is called an optional hyphen, which will print only if it occurs at the end of a line.*

Hyphenate Automatically

1. Place insertion point where hyphenation will begin.

2. Click **T**o**ols** menu .... `Alt` + `O`

3. Click **H**yphenation .... `H`

4. Click **C**onfirm checkbox .... `C`
   to clear (☐).

5. Click Hot **Z**one text box .... `Z`

6. Type desired width .... *number*

   NOTE: *The smaller the zone, the less ragged the margin.*

6. Click **OK** .... `↵`

Hyphenate with Confirm

1. Place insertion point where hyphenation will begin.

2. Click **T**o**ols** menu .... `Alt` + `O`

3. Click **H**yphenation .... `H`

4. Click **C**onfirm checkbox .... `C`
   to select (☒).

5. Click Hot **Z**one text box .... `Z`

6. Type desired width .... *number*

   NOTE: *The smaller the zone, the less ragged the margin.*

(continued...)

HYPHENATE WITH CONFIRM (continued)

7. Click **OK**.. ⏎

Word to be hyphenated appears in the dialog box.

8. Choose one of the following options:

    • Click **Yes**.. **Alt** + **Y**
      to accept suggested hyphenation.

    • Click **No**... **Alt** + **N**
      to avoid hyphenating word.

    • Press arow keys... **←** , **→**
      to move position of hyphen.

    • Click **Cancel**.. **Esc**
      to cancel hyphenation.

Remove Optional Hyphens

1. Click **Edit** menu...................................... **Alt** + **E**

2. Click **Replace** .... **L**

3. Click **Find What** text box .... **Alt** , **N**

4. Type .... **^** , **-**

5. Clear **Replace With** text box.............. **Alt** + **P** , **Del**
    if necessary.

6. Click **Find Next** .... **Alt** + **F**

(continued...)

REMOVE OPTIONAL HYPHENS (continued)

7. Click **Replace** .... R
   to remove hyphen.

   OR

   Click **Find Next** .... F
   to find next hyphen.

8. Repeat step 7 until finished.

9. Click **Close** .... Esc

CREATE PARAGRAPH BORDERS

1. Select paragraph(s) to border.

2. Click **Format** menu .... Alt + T

3. Click **Border** .... B

4. Click desired border positions from the following options:

   • Outline .... O

   • Top .... Alt + T

   • Bottom .... M

   • Left L

   • Right .... R

5. Click desired **Line style** option from the following:

   • Normal .... N

   • Bold .... B

   • Double .... D

(continued...)

CREATE PARAGRAPH BORDERS (continued)

6. Click desired **C**olor.. `C` , `↓`

7. Click **OK**.. `↵`

Remove Borders

1. Select paragraphs to clear.

2. Click **Forma**t menu .... `Alt` + `T`

3. Click **B**order... `B`

4. Click undesired border positions to clear check box (□).

5. Click **OK**.. `↵`

FIND AND REPLACE

See REPLACE, page 62.

Find Text

Operates from insertion point to the end of the document.

1. Place insertion point where search will begin.

2. Click **E**dit menu... `Alt` + `E`

3. Click **F**ind... `F`

4. Click **Fi**nd **What:** .... `Alt` + `N`

5. Type text for search ....*text*

   NOTE: Use ? for wildcard.

(continued...)

FIND TEXT (continued)

6. Click additional desired criteria to select (⊠) if desired:

- Match <u>W</u>hole Word Only .... `Alt` + `W`

- Match <u>C</u>ase .... `Alt` + `C`

7. Click <u>F</u>ind next .... `Alt` + `F`

8. Repeat step 7, if desired.

9. Click **Cancel** .... `Esc`
   when finished.

Repeat a Search

Press .... `F7`

Find and Replace Text

Finds specific instances of text or special characters in a document, then replaces it with other text or characters.

1. Place insertion point where search will to begin.

2. Click <u>E</u>dit menu .... `Alt` + `E`

3. Click <u>R</u>eplace .... `R`

4. Click Fi<u>n</u>d What: .... `Alt` + `N`

5. Type text for search .... *text*

   NOTE: Use ? for wildcard.

6. Click Re<u>p</u>lace With: .... `Alt` + `P`

7. Type new text .... *text*

(continued...)

FIND AND REPLACE TEXT (continued)

8. Click additional desired criteria to select (⊠) if desired:

   • Match Whole Word Only .... `Alt` + `W`

   • Match Case .... `Alt` + `C`

9. Click Find next .... `Alt` + `F`

10. Click Replace .... `Alt` + `R`

   NOTE: Works will pause at each occurrence of matched text.

   OR

   Click **Replace All** .... `Alt` + `A`

   NOTE: Works will replace all occurrences of matched text.

   OR

   Click Find next .... `Alt` + `F`

11. Click **Close** .... `Alt` + `E`
    when finished.

Find and Replace Special Characters

*The following codes are used to find and replace special characters. The codes may be used in combination with text in the **Find What** and **Replace With** text boxes.*

Any character .... `?`

Caret (^) .... `^` `^`

End-of-line mark .... `^` `N`

(continued...)

FIND AND REPLACE SPECIAL CHARACTERS (continued)

Nonbreaking space	`^` `S`
Page-break mark	`^` `D`
Paragraph mark	`^` `P`
Question mark	`^` `?`
Tab mark	`^` `T`
White space	`^` `W`

CREATE FOOTNOTES

Footnotes are notes documenting text, placed at the bottom of the pages of a document. Corresponding superscript numbers (or characters) are placed in the text, following the referenced item.

The Footnote Works Wizard will help format footnotes for a variety of reference sources.

1. Place insertion point where footnote reference is intended to appear.

2. Click **Insert** menu .... `Alt` + `I`

3. Click **Footnote** .... `T`

4. Choose one of the following options:

   Numbered .... `Alt` + `N`

   OR

   a. Click **Character mark** .... `Alt` + `C`

(continued...)

CREATE FOOTNOTES (continued)

    b. Click <u>M</u>ark .... `Alt` + `M`

    c. Type character to display .... *character*

5. Click <u>U</u>se Works Wizard, ... `Alt` + `U`
    if desired.

    NOTE: Follow instructions on screen.

    OR

    a. Click **OK** .... `⏎`

    b. Type footnote in footnote pane.

6. Click document pane to return to document .... `F6`

Open or Close Footnote Pane

1. Click <u>V</u>iew menu .... `Alt` + `V`

2. Click <u>F</u>ootnotes .... `F`
    to select (✔) or deselect.

Edit Footnote

1. Open footnote pane *(see above)*.

2. Click footnote pane.

    OR

    Press .... `F6`

3. Edit text as in a document window.

4. Click document pane.

    OR

    Press .... `F6`

Delete Footnote Reference Mark

– IN DOCUMENT WINDOW –

1. Select footnote mark to delete.

2. Press .... `Del`

Move or Copy Footnote Reference Mark

– IN DOCUMENT WINDOW –

1. Select footnote mark to move.

2. Click **E**dit menu... `Alt` + `E`

3. Click **Cut** .... `T`

   OR

   Click **C**opy.. `C`

4. Place insertion point where new footnote mark will appear.

5. Click **E**dit menu... `Alt` + `E`

6. Click **P**aste .... `P`

Change Footnote Mark

1. Select footnote mark to change in either document or footnote pane.

2. Click **I**nsert menu.. `Alt` + `I`

3. Click **Foo**t**note** .... `T`

4. Click **C**haracter mark................................. `Alt` + `C`

5. Click **M**ark.. `Alt` + `M`

6. Type desired character.............................. *character*

7. Click **OK**.. `↵`

Specify Footnote Location

Footnotes may be printed at the bottom of each page, or at the end of a document as endnotes.

1. Click **F**ile menu.. `Alt` + `F`

2. Click **P**age Setup... `G`

3. Click **O**ther Options tab .... `Alt` + `O`

4. Click **P**rint Footnotes at End of Document .... `Alt` + `R`
    to select (☒) or clear (☐).

5. Click **OK**... `↵`

CREATE COLUMNS

> *NOTE:* *Columns are used for entire documents only. To create headlines across a columned page, use paragraph headers (see page 55). Columns must be viewed in Page Layout mode (see page 27).*

1. Click **Forma**t menu .... `Alt` + `T`

2. Click **C**olumns .... `C`

– IN NUMBER OF COLUMNS TEXT BOX –

3. Click **N**umber of Columns text box .... `Alt` + `N`

4. Type number desired ....*number*

5. Select **S**pace between text box...................... `Alt` + `S`

6. Type space between columns.

7. Click **L**ine Between .... `Alt` + `L`
    to select (☒), if desired.

8. Click **OK**... `↵`

9. Click **OK**... `↵`
    to view in Page Layout mode.

Remove Columns

1. Click **Format** menu .... `Alt` + `T`

2. Click **Columns** .... `C`

3. Click **Number of Columns** text box .... `Alt` + `N`

3. Type **1** .... `1`

4. Click **OK** .... `↵`

INSERT SPREADSHEET TABLE

1. Place insertion point where spreadsheet will appear.

2. Click **Insert** menu .... `Alt` + `I`

3. Click **Spreadsheet/Table** .... `P`

4. Click **New Table** .... `N`

5. Click **OK** .... `↵`

6. Type desired information into table
   (see spreadsheet section, page 87).

   To make larger or smaller:

   Click and drag corner or side of table.

   To return to word processing document:

   Click document

   OR

   Press.. `Esc`

   To return to table:

   Double-click table.

INSERT BOOKMARKS

A bookmark is a hidden, named marker, helpful for quickly locating a place in a document.

1. Place insertion point where bookmark is to be located.

2. Click **I**nsert menu.. `Alt` + `I`

3. Click **Bookmark N**ame .... `N`

4. Click **N**ame: .... `Alt` + `N`

5. Type desired name..*text*

6. Click **OK**... `↵`

Go to a Bookmark or Page

1. Press .... `F5`

   OR

   a. Click **E**dit menu... `Alt` + `E`

   b. Click **G**o to .... `G`

2. Type bookmark name or page number ....*text*

   OR

   a. Click **N**ames list box .... `Alt` + `N`

   b. Select bookmark name.. `↓`

3. Click **OK**... `↵`

Delete a Bookmark

1. Click **I**nsert menu.. `Alt` + `I`

2. Click **Bookmark N**ame .... `N`

(continued...)

DELETE A BOOKMARK (continued)

3. Click **Names** list box .... `Alt` + `S`

4. Select bookmark name .... `↓`

5. Click **Delete** .... `Alt` + `T`

6. Click **Close** .... `Alt` + `C`

INSERT SPECIAL CHARACTERS

Display or Hide Special Characters

1. Click **View** menu .... `Alt` + `V`

2. Click **All Characters** .... `L`

Insert Special Characters

1. Place insertion point where character is to be positioned.

2. Choose desired special character:

   • Paragraph mark () .... `↵`

   • Tab mark () .... `Tab`

   • Space mark ( ) .... `Space`

   • End-of-line mark ( ) .... `Shift` + `↵`

Insert Any Special Character

1. Place insertion point where character is to be positioned.

2. Click **Insert** menu .... `I`

(continued...)

INSERT ANY SPECIAL CHARACTER (continued)

3. Click **Special Character** .... S

4. Click desired character to select from the following options:

   • End-of-line mark.. L
     to create a new line.

   • Optional hyphen .... O
     to hyphenate a word, if necessary.

   • Non-breaking hyphen.. Y
     to keep hyphenated words from breaking
     at the end of a line.

   • Non-breaking space .... S
     to keep two words from breaking
     at the end of a line.

   • Print page number.. P
     to insert placeholder for page number.

   • Print filename .... F
     to insert placeholder for filename.

   • Print date .... D
     to insert placeholder for date.

   • Print long date.. N
     to insert placeholder for long format date.

   • Print time.. T
     to insert placeholder for current time.

   • Current date.. C
     to insert current date.

   • Current time.. U
     to insert current time.

5. Click **OK**... ↵

CREATE AND PRINT MAILING LABELS

NOTE: *The word processor can be used to print mailing labels from the names and addresses in any database. Preset dimensions are available for common formats.*

Create Mailing Label Document

1. Create and close database containing name and addresses *(see Database Section, page 155)*.

2. Click **F**ile menu..`Alt` + `F`

3. Click **Create New File**..`N`

4. Click **W**ord Processor button...............................`W`

5. Click **T**ools menu..`Alt` + `O`

6. Click **Envelopes and Labels**...............................`E`

7. Click **M**ailing Labels tab.....................................`Alt` + `M`

8. Click **F**ields button..`Alt` + `F`

   To name database to use:

   Click **Datab**ase button.......................................`Alt` + `B`

9. Select database to use...`↓`

10. Click **OK**..`↵`

11. Click **F**ields list box...`Alt` + `F`

12. Select first field to include...................................`↓`
    from **Fields** list box.

(continued...)

CREATE MAILING LABEL DOCUMENT (continued)

13. Click **Insert** button .... `Alt` + `I`

14. Repeat steps 11 to 13 for each additional field to include.

– IN LABEL BOX –

15. Type any formatting, punctuation or text
    to include on each label before, after or in
    between field placeholders.

– FOR STANDARD SIZE LABELS –

Select label from **Label Style** box .... `Alt` + `S`

OR

– FOR CUSTOM SIZE LABELS –

a. Click **Custom Label** button .... `Alt` + `U`

b. Type number of labels .... *number*
   Across page.

c. Press .... `Tab`

d. Type number of labels.. *number*
   Down page.

e. Press .... `Tab`

f. Type **Horizontal** label measurement..................... *number*

g. Press .... `Tab`

h. Type **Vertical** label measurement......................... *number*

i. Click **OK**.. `↵`

(continued...)

CREATE MAILING LABEL DOCUMENT (continued)

j. Type **L**eft margin of page .... *number*

k. Press .... `Tab`

l. Type **T**op margin of page .... *number*

m.Click **W**idth text box.............................. `Alt` + `W`

n. Type width measurement..................................... *number*

o. Click **L**ength text box .... `Alt` + `E`

p. Type length measurement..................................... *number*

q. Click **L**andscape orientation .... `Alt` + `L`
   if desired

r. Click **OK**.. `←`

16. Click **C**reate **Label** button .... `Alt` + `C`

17. Press.. `Ctrl` + `S`
    to save and name document (see page 5).

Preview Mailing Labels

1. View document containing label placeholders.

2. Click **F**ile menu................................ `Alt` + `F`

3. Click **Print Preview** .... `V`

4. Select database from list box................................. `↓`

5. Click **OK**.. `←`

6. Click **OK** to merge records .... `←`

(continued...)

PREVIEW MAILING LABELS (continued)

7. Click **Print** .... `Alt` + `P`
   when finished viewing labels
   (see Print Preview, page 20).

   OR

   Click **Cancel** .... `Esc`
   to return to document.

Modify Mailing Labels

1. View mailing label document.

2. Using standard editing and formatting
   features to make changes to placeholders.

3. Click **Tools** menu .... `Alt` + `O`

4. Click **Envelopes and Labels** .... `E`

5. Click **Mailing Labels** tab .... `Alt` + `M`

6. Make desired changes following directions above.

7. Click **Change Label** .... `Alt` + `C`

Print Labels

1. View label document to print.

2. Load label paper in printer.

3. Click **File** menu .... `Alt` + `F`

4. Click **Print** .... `P`

5. Click **Mailing Labels** button .... `Alt` + `N`

(continued...)

76

PRINT LABELS (continued)

6. Click **Print Merge** check box .... `Alt` + `I`

7. Click **OK**.. `↵`

   OR

   Click **Test** .... `Alt` + `E`
   to print first row only.

8. Select desired database from list .... `↓`

9. Click **OK**.. `↵`

   NOTE: If necessary, click OK again to merge.

CREATE FORM LETTERS

*Prints copies of the same document with different information
inserted from selected fields of a database.*

1. Create database file with variable information
   such as names and addresses *(see page 155)*.

2. Create word processing document (a letter, for example).

3. Place insertion point in word processing
   document where first database field
   placeholder will appear.

4. Click **Insert** menu.............................. `Alt` + `I`

5. Click **Database Field**................................. `F`

6. Click **Databases** list box .... `Alt` + `B`

7. Select database to use ...., `↓`

(continued...)

CREATE FORM LETTERS (continued)

8. Click **OK**... ⏎

9. Click **Fields** list box .... Alt + F

10. Select field to place .... ↓

11. Click **Insert**... Alt + I

12. Repeat steps 10 and 11 for each field to place.

13. Click **Close** button .... Alt + E
    when finished adding fields.

– IN WORD PROCESSING WINDOW –

14. Type any formatting, punctuation or text to
    include on each label before, after or in between
    field placeholders.

15. Press... Ctrl + S
    to save document.

Modify Form Letter

1. View form letter document.

2. Make changes to placeholders using standard editing and
    formatting features.

3. Click **Insert** menu... Alt + I

4. Make desired changes following instructions above.

5. Click **Close** .... E
    when finished.

6. Press... Ctrl + S
    to save document.

USE CHARTS, DRAWINGS, AND OTHER OBJECTS IN DOCUMENTS

There are several ways to incorporate charts, drawings and other objects in word processing documents. Objects may be copied (and later deleted), linked (and remain joined to the file from which they were copied and are updated when the original is updated) or embedded (the original application may be launched from the word processor).

LINK OBJECTS

Link Spreadsheet Chart to Document

> *NOTE: Linked charts will be automatically updated when the source spreadsheet is updated.*

1. View spreadsheet with chart to link.

2. View word processing document in second window.

– IN WORD PROCESSING WINDOW –

3. Place insertion point where you wish to place linked chart.

4. Click **Insert** menu... **Alt** + **I**

5. Click **Chart**... **C**

6. Click **Use existing chart** .... **Alt** + **U**

7. Select desired **Spreadsheet**................. **Alt** + **S** , ↓

8. Select desired **Chart**............................. **Alt** + **S** , ↓

10. Click **OK**.. ↵

Link a Spreadsheet Range to a Document

> *NOTE: Linked spreadsheet ranges will be automatically updated when the source spreadsheet is updated.*

(continued...)

LINK SPREADSHEET CHART TO DOCUMENT (continued)

1. Open spreadsheet with desired range.

   NOTE: *Spreadsheet must be named and saved, and range must be named.*

2. View word processing document to which you wish to add spreadsheet range.

   – IN WORD PROCESSING WINDOW –

3. Place insertion point at desired location.

4. Click **Insert** menu..`Alt` + `I`

5. Click **Spread/Table** ....`P`

6. Click **Use existing chart** ....`Alt` + `U`

7. Select desired **Spreadsheet**..................`Alt` + `S`, `↓`

8. Select desired **Range** ....`Alt` + `R`, `↓`

9. Click **OK**...`↵`

Change a Link to a Manual Link

   NOTE: *Manual links will be updated only on command.*

1. View word processing document to change.

2. Click **Edit** menu..`Alt` + `E`

3. Click **Links**...`K`

4. Select linked object ....`↓`
   to change.

5. Click **Manual** ....`M`

6. Click **Close** button ....`Esc`

80

Update a Manual Link

1. Click **Edit** menu.. **Alt** + **E**

2. Click **Links**.. **K**

3. Select linked object .... **↓**
   to update.

4. Click **Update Now**.. **Alt** + **U**

5. Click **Close** button... **Esc**

Link Objects from Other Windows Applications

1. View file with object to link.

2. Select text, cells, drawing or area to link.

3. Press.. **Ctrl** + **C**

4. View word processing document to receive object.

5. Place insertion point.

6. Click **Edit** menu.. **Alt** + **E**

7. Click **Paste Special**... **S**

8. Click **Paste Link** .... **L**

9. Click **OK**.. **↵**

EMBED OBJECTS

Embed a Spreadsheet

When an object is embedded, it remains attached to the application that created it (the application must be installed on the hard drive). The object may be edited from the word processor.

1. Place insertion point at desired location.

2. Click **Insert** menu.. `Alt` + `I`

3. Click **Spreadsheet/Table** .... `P`

4. Click **New Table**.. `Alt` + `N`

5. Click **OK**.. `↵`

6. Type desired information *(see page 87)*.

   To change size of spreadsheet:

   Click and drag corner to new location.

   To return to word processor:

   Click document

   OR

   Press.. `Esc`

Embed a Chart

1. Place insertion point at desired location.

2. Click **Insert** menu.. `Alt` + `I`

3. Click **Chart**.. `C`

4. Click **OK**.. `↵`

(continued...)

EMBED A CHART (continued)

5. Enter values for chart in spreadsheet.

6. Click **Chart** button (lower left corner).

7. Choose chart options *(see page 127)*.

8. Click **OK**... `⏎`

    To return to word processor:

    Click document.

    OR

    Press... `Esc`

Embed ClipArt, a Drawing, Note-It or WordArt

1. Place insertion point at desired location.

2. Click **I**nsert menu...................................... `Alt` + `I`

3. Choose desired object type from the following options:

    • ClipArt.. `A`

    • **W**ordArt.. `W`

    • Not**e**-It... `E`

    • Draw**i**ng .... `I`

4. Select or create object in tool or application.

5. Quit application or tool by pressing escape,
    or use the file menu to quit and return to
    document window.

Embed Other Object

1. Place insertion point at desired location.

2. Click **I**nsert menu.. `Alt` + `I`

3. Click **O**bject .... `O`

4. Choose object to create:

   a. Click **Create New** .... `Alt` + `N`

   b. Click **Object Type** .... `Alt` + `T`, `↓`

   OR

   a. Click **Create from File** .... `Alt` + `F`

   b. Type **File** name in text box .... `Alt` + `E`

5. Click **OK**.. `↵`

EDIT OBJECT

Double-click object.

OR

1. Move insertion point to left of object .... `←`

2. Press.. `Shift` + `→`

CHANGE OBJECT SIZE

1. Click object to change.

2. Drag handle to desired size.

   *NOTE: Handles are squares that appear at each corner and
   in the center of each edge of a selected object.*

Resize Object Precisely

1. Click object to resize.

2. Click **Format** menu .... `Alt` + `T`

3. Click **Picture/Object** .... `U`

4. Click **Size** tab .... `Alt` + `S`

5. Click **Width** text box .... `Alt` + `W`

6. Type new width .... *number*

7. Click **Height** text box .... `Alt` + `H`

8. Type new height .... *number*

9. Click Scaling **Width** text box .... `Alt` + `I`

10. Type new width scale .... *number*

11. Click Scaling **Height** text box .... `Alt` + `E`

12. Type new height scale .... *number*

13. Click **OK** .... `←`

Move Object

1.   Click object to move.

   OR

   a. Move insertion point to left of object .... `←`

   b. Press .... `Shift` + `→`

2.   Drag object to new position.

   OR

   a. Click **E**dit menu .... `Alt` + `E`

   b. Click C**u**t .... `U`

   c. Move insertion point to new position.

   d. Click **E**dit menu .... `Alt` + `E`

   e. Click **P**aste .... `P`

Wrap Text Around Object

   NOTE: Use Text Wrap to continue text on left or right of page next to embedded object.

1.   Click object to select.

2.   Click **Forma**t menu .... `Alt` + `T`

3.   Click Pict**u**re/Object .... `U`

4.   Click **T**ext Wrap tab .... `Alt` + `T`

5.   Click **A**bsolute .... `A`
   to wrap text completely around object.

(continued...)

WRAP TEXT AROUND OBJECT (continued)

6. Click desired option.............................. `Alt` + `O`, `↓`
   in H**o**rizontal list box.

7. Click desired option .... `Alt` + `V`, `↓`
   in **V**ertical list box.

8. Click **OK**.. `↵`

9. Click **Yes**... `Y`
   to view object in Page Layout view.

Spreadsheet

THE SPREADSHEET WINDOW

Cell reference   Cancel   Enter   Formula   Column labels

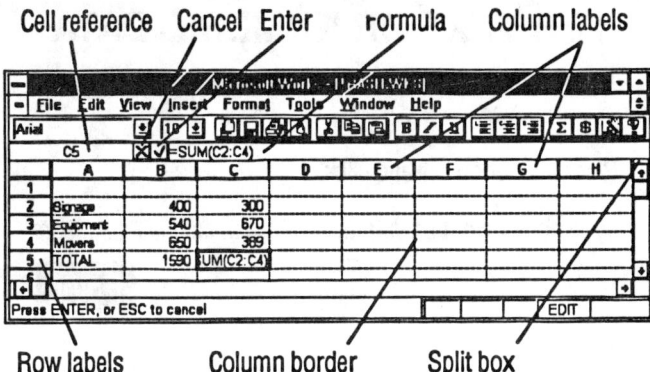

Row labels   Column border   Split box

SHOW OR HIDE CELL GRIDLINES

1. Click **View** menu...**Alt** + **V**

2. Click **Gridlines**...**G**

KEEP ROW AND COLUMN TITLES ON SCREEN (FREEZE)

> *NOTE: Freezing titles affects all rows and columns above
> and to the left of the highlight.*

1. Select cell below and to right of columns and rows to freeze.

2. Click **Format** menu ....**Alt** + **T**

3. Click **Freeze Titles** ....**T**

(continued...)

Unfreeze Rows and Columns

1. Click **Format** menu .... `Alt` + `T`

2. Click **Freeze Titles** .... `T`
   to deselect.

ENTER TEXT OR NUMERIC DATA

> *NOTE:* *Data appears in the cell and the formula bar as you type.*

1. Place pointer on cell and click.

2. Type numeric or text data ....*data*

3. Press .... `Enter`

   OR

   Click.. ☑

ENTER FORMULA

A formula is an equation using numbers that have been entered in other cells of the spreadsheet. For example: B2 + 5 or 8 * (C12/2 + 6). (See Enter Formula Using Operators, page 100 and Enter Formula Using Functions, page 104.) The formula appears in the cell and the formula bar as you type.

1. Place pointer on cell and click.

2. Type... `=`

3. Type formula ....*formula*

4. Click.. ☑

   OR

   Press .... `Enter`

TOTAL QUICKLY

1. Select cell at end of row or column to total.

2. Click .... $\boxed{\Sigma}$

    OR

    Press .... $\boxed{\text{Ctrl}}$ + $\boxed{\text{M}}$

3. Press .... $\boxed{\text{Enter}}$

    OR

    Click .... $\boxed{\checkmark}$

    *NOTE: If there is a blank cell in the row or column to total,
    Works will only select cells to total from the
    beginning of the range to the blank cell. To total
    more cells, manually select them (see page 91).*

MOVE AROUND IN SPREADSHEET

Scroll Through Spreadsheet

*Lets you view different parts of a spreadsheet too large to fit on
one screen. Scrolling does not move the insertion point.*

Click scroll bar .... $\boxed{\uparrow}$ $\boxed{\downarrow}$
until desired screen appears.

Move Insertion Point Using Keyboard

One cell left .... $\boxed{\leftarrow}$

One cell right .... $\boxed{\rightarrow}$

One row up .... $\boxed{\uparrow}$

One row down .... $\boxed{\downarrow}$

MOVE INSERTION POINT USING KEYBOARD (continued)

Beginning of row .... `Home`

Last column with data .... `End`

Beginning of spreadsheet .... `Ctrl` + `Home`

Last row or column with data .... `Ctrl` + `End`

One window up .... `PgUp`

One window down .... `PgDn`

Left one window .... `Ctrl` + `PgUp`

Right one window .... `Ctrl` + `PgDn`

Between panes of split window .... `F6`

Go to Cell or Range

1. Press .... `F5`

2. Type cell address, range name or range reference in
   go to dialog box.

   OR

   Select name .... `N`, `↓`
   from **Name** list box.

3. Click **OK** .... `Enter`

SELECT OR HIGHLIGHT CELLS

Select One Cell

Place pointer over cell and click.

OR

Press.. ← → ↑ ↓
to highlight desired cell.

Select Row

Place pointer over row number and click.

OR

a. Move to a cell in desired row.............. ← → ↑ ↓

b. Press.. Ctrl + F8

Select a Column

Place pointer over column letter and click.

OR

a. Move cell in desired column................ ← → ↑ ↓

b. Press .... Shift + F8

Select a Group (Range) of Cells

1. Click corner cell of group and drag to opposite corner.

2. Release mouse button.

OR

1. Move to corner cell of group.

2. Press F8

3. Move to opposite corner cell .... ← → ↑ ↓

Select Large Group of Cells

1. Click corner cell of group to select.

2. Press .... `F8`

3. Press .... `F5`

4. Type cell address .... *address*
   of opposite corner group to select.

5. Click **OK**.. `Enter`

Select Entire Spreadsheet

Place pointer over box to left of column A and above row 1 and click.

OR

Press.. `Ctrl` + `Shift` + `F8`

Cancel Selection

Click anywhere in spreadsheet.

EDIT CELL CONTENTS

Clear Cells

1. Select cell(s) to clear.

2. Press .... `Del`

Type over Cell Entry

1. Select cell to change.

2. Type new entry.. *data*

3. Press .... `Enter`

   OR

   Click.. ☑

Change Cell Entry

1. Select cell to change.

2. Click formula bar.

   OR

   Press .... `F2`

3. Choose one of the following options to change contents:

   - Place insertion point at beginning of text......... `Home`

   - Click to left of first character in line.

   - Place insertion point at end of text..................... `End`

   - Click to right of last character in line.

   - Move insertion point left or right .... `←`, `→`
     (repeat as desired)

   - Click at desired position.

   - Click and drag over characters to select

   - Press........................... `Shift` + `→`, `Shift` + `←`

   - Delete selected characters....................................... `Del`

4. Press .... `Enter`
   when editing is complete.

   OR

   Click... ☑

DRAG AND DROP

Cell contents may be moved by the drag and drop method from one place to another in a spreadsheet, or from one Works or Windows file to another. If information is dragged from another application to the spreadsheet, it will probably be automatically embedded (see page 67).

Drag and Drop to Move Cell Contents

If moving cell contents from one file to another:

1. Arrange screen to view both windows.

2. Select cell or cells to move.

3. Place insertion point on edge of selection.

4. Press and hold mouse button.

    If dragging between documents or application:

    Hold .... Shift

5. Drag selection to new location.

    NOTE: Insertion point will change appearance to indicate selection is being dragged. If insertion point changes to a circle with a slash, it indicates that the selection cannot be moved to that location with this method.

6. Release mouse button and shift key.

Drag and Drop to Copy Cell Contents

If moving cell contents from one file to another:

1. Arrange screen to view both windows.

2. Select cell(s) to copy.

3. Place insertion point on edge of selection.

(continued...)

DRAG AND DROP TO COPY CELL CONTENTS (continued)

4. Hold .... Ctrl
   unless dragging between
   documents or applications.

5. Hold mouse button.

6. Drag selection to new location.

   *NOTE: Insertion point will change appearance to indicate
   selection is being dragged. If insertion point
   changes to a circle with a slash, it indicates that the
   selection can not be moved to that location with
   this method.*

7. Release mouse button and shift key.

CUT, COPY AND PASTE

Copy Cell Contents

1. Select cell(s) to copy.

2. Press .... Ctrl + Ins

   OR

   a. Click **E**dit menu .... Alt + E

   b. Click **C**opy C

3. Select cell at upper-left corner of area to receive copied cells.

4. Press .... Shift + Ins

   OR

   a. Click **E**dit menu .... Alt + E

   b. Click **P**aste .... P

Cut and Paste Cell Contents

1. Select cell(s) to cut and paste.

2. Press... `Ctrl` + `Del`

   OR

   a. Click **E**dit menu .... `Alt` + `E`

   b. Click **Cu**t... `T`

3. Select cell at upper-left corner of area to receive moved cells.

4. Press... `Shift` + `Ins`

   OR

   a. Click **E**dit menu .... `Alt` + `E`

   b. Click **P**aste... `P`

Repeat Paste Command with Same Data

1. Select cell at upper-left corner of area to receive cells.

2. Press... `Shift` + `Ins`

   OR

   a. Click **E**dit menu .... `Alt` + `E`

   b. Click **P**aste .... `Alt` + `P`

Copy to Neighboring Cells

Cell contents may be copied to cells below or to the right with this method.

1. Select cells to copy as well as additional neighboring area where data will be repeated.

(continued...)

COPY TO NEIGHBORING CELLS (continued)

2. Click **E**dit menu.. `Alt` + `E`

3. Click **Fill R**ight.. `R`

   OR

   Click **Fill D**o**w**n.. `W`

Copy, Add or Subtract Values Only

Copies, adds or subtracts only the resulting value of a formula, not the formula itself.

1. Select cell(s) to copy.

2. Click **E**dit menu.. `Alt` + `E`

3. Click **C**opy... `C`

4. Select cell at upper-left corner of area to receive copied cells.

5. Click **E**dit menu.. `Alt` + `E`

6. Click **Paste S**pecial... `S`

7. Choose one of the following options:

   • **V**alues only.. `V`

   • **A**dd values.. `A`

   NOTE: Adds values to selected cells.

   • **S**ubtract values.. `S`

   NOTE: Subtracts values from selected cells.

8. Click **OK**.. `Enter`

NAMING CELLS OR GROUPS OF CELLS

Cells or groups of cells may be named and names may be used in formulas, searches, or to reference the cell or cells in a chart.

Name Cell or Range

1. Select cell(s) to name.

2. Click **I**nsert menu.. `Alt` + `I`

3. Click **Range Name** .... `N`

4. Type range name .... *name*

   OR

   Accept suggested name.

5. Click **OK**.. `Enter`

Select Named Range

1. Click **E**dit menu.. `Alt` + `E`

2. Click **G**o to .... `G`

3. Click **N**ames.. `Alt` + `N`

4. Select desired name.. `↓`

5. Click **OK**.. `Enter`

Delete Range Name

1. Click **I**nsert menu.. `Alt` + `I`

2. Click **Range Name** .... `N`

(continued...)

DELETE RANGE NAME (continued)

3. Click **Names**... Alt + S

4. Select name... ↓
   to delete.

5. Click **Delete** .... Alt + T

6. Click **Close**... Alt + C

Change Range Reference

1. Select cell(s) for new range.

2. Click **Insert** menu.. Alt + I

3. Click **Range Name** .... N

4. Click **Names**.. Alt + S

5. Select name... ↓
   to reassign.

6. Click **OK**... Enter

Use a Range Name in Formula

1. Select cell to contain formula.

2. Type formula up to range or cell reference.

3. Type name of range...*range name*
   to reference.

4. Finish typing formula...*formula*

5. Press .... Enter

   OR

   Click.. ☑

Display a List of Range Names in Spreadsheet

1. Select upper-left cell of group to contain list.

2. Click **I**nsert menu .... `Alt` + `I`

3. Click **Range Name** .... `N`

4. Click **L**ist .... `Alt` + `L`

OPERATORS

Operators are listed in order of their evaluation by Works. Works follows standard algebraic rules to evaluate formulas.

Parentheses ....( )

Negative and positive numbers...-, +

Exponentials ....^

Multiplication, division .... *, /

Addition, subtraction.. + , -

Comparison operators ....=, <>, <, >, <=, >=

NOT ....~

OR, AND..|, &

Enter Formula Using Operators

1. Select cell to contain formula.

2. Type.. `=`

(continued...)

ENTER FORMULA USING OPERATORS (continued)

3. Type cell reference............................*cell reference or number*
    or number.

Example: A4

4. Type operator...*operator*

Example: +

5. Type cell reference............................*cell reference or number*
    or number.

6. Repeat steps 3 and 4, as needed.

7. Press .... Enter

    OR

    Click.. ✓

Enter a Formula Using Functions

NOTE: For a list of built-in functions, see the APPENDIX, p. 261.

1. Select cell to contain formula.

2. Type.. =

3. Type function...*function*

Example: COUNT

    OR

    a. Click Insert menu.............................. Alt + I

    b. Click Function... F

(continued...)

102

ENTER A FORMULA USING FUNCTIONS (continued)

c. Choose one of the following options:

- <u>A</u>ll .... `A`
- Fi<u>n</u>ancial .... `N`
- <u>D</u>ate and Time .... `D`
- <u>M</u>ath and Trig .... `M`
- <u>S</u>tatistical .... `S`
- L<u>o</u>okup and Ref .... `O`
- <u>T</u>ext .... `T`
- <u>L</u>ogical .... `L`
- <u>I</u>nformational .... `I`

d. Click desired <u>F</u>unction .... `Alt` + `F`
   from list box.

*NOTE: In the list box, press the first letter of the function
         to quickly see it. A description of the function
         appears at the bottom of the Insert Function dialog
         box.*

e. Click **OK** .... `Enter`

4. Type .... `(`

5. Type desired numbers .... *number, cell reference*
   or cell references separated
   by commas.

6. Type .... `)`

7. Press .... `Enter`

   OR

   Click .... `☑`

USE RANGE IN FORMULA

A range is a group of adjacent cells. One-column ranges or one-row ranges frequently appear in formulas that use the SUM or AVG functions.

1. Select cell to contain formula.

2. Type..

3. Type function...*function*

EXAMPLE: SUM

4. Click and drag to select range.

   OR

   Type..*first cell:last cell*

5. Press .... Enter

   OR

   Click.. ☑

CELL REFERENCES

Use Relative References for Cells and Ranges

> *NOTE:* *When a simple cell reference, such as A4 or B8 (column and row, respectively), is used in a formula, it is seen by Works as a relative reference. If a formula containing a relative reference is copied or moved, the reference will point to a new location in the same relative distances from the cell containing the formula.*

1. Select cell to contain formula.

2. Type formula up to cell reference.

(continued...)

USE RELATIVE REFERENCES FOR CELLS AND RANGES (continued)

3. Type cell column letter followed by cell row number.

    OR

    Select cell(s) to include.

4. Finish typing formula.

5. Click.. ☑

    OR

    Press .... Enter

Use Absolute References for Cells and Ranges

Use absolute references in formulas if you want a formula to always point to the same cell, even if the formula is moved or copied. To make a cell reference absolute, insert a dollar sign before either or both parts of the cell reference.

Example: A4 will always point to cell A4. A$4 will always point to the fourth row, but the reference to column A is relative, and will change if the formula is moved or copied. $A4 will always point to column A but the reference to row 4 is relative.

Insert Absolute Reference

1. Select cell to contain formula.

2. Type formula ....*formula*
    up to cell reference.

3. Type cell reference................................*cell reference*
    including $ signs.

    OR

    a. Select cell or range of cells to include in cell reference.

(continued...)

INSERT ABSOLUTE REFERENCE (continued)

    b. Press.. `F4`
       until desired reference combination appears in
       formula bar.

5.   Type remainder of formula.

6.   Press .... `Enter`

   OR

   Click... ✓

Show or Hide Formulas

1.   Click <u>V</u>iew menu.............................. `Alt` + `V`

2.   Click <u>F</u>ormulas.. `F`
   to select (◉) or deselect.

USE DATES AND TIMES FOR REFERENCES AND CALCULATIONS

*Dates and times may be used in formulas, references, calculations,
and in cells. They must be typed in Works formats.*

Date and Time Formats

Long Examples

Month, day, year...July 23, 1993

Month, year...July 1993

Month, day..July 23

Month July ....July

(continued...)

DATE AND TIME FORMATS (continued)

Short Examples

Month, day, year 7/23/93

Month, year 7/93

Month, day 7/23

24-hour

Hour, minute, second...16:30:00

Hour, minute 16:30

12-hour

Hour, minute, second ....4:30:00 AM

Hour, minute...4:30 AM

ENTER DATE OR TIME

1. Place insertion point where date or time is to appear.

2. Type date or time using a Works format.

3. Press .... Enter

    OR

    Click..☑

    Date or time will automatically be displayed in previously selected format.

Change Date or Time Format

1. Select cell or range to change.

(continued...)

CHANGE DATE AND TIME FORMAT (continued)

2. Click **Format** menu .... `Alt` + `T`

3. Click **Number** .... `N`

4. Click **Date** .... `D`

   OR

   Click **Time** .... `Alt` + `T`

5. Select desired format .... `↓`
   from **Options** list box.

6. Click **OK** .... `Enter`

Insert Current Date or Time (Non-Recalculating)

Inserts the date or time, which will not change if you recalculate the spreadsheet.

1. Select cell where date or time is intended to appear.

2. Press .... `Ctrl` + `;`
   to enter current date

   OR

   Press .... `Ctrl` + `Shift` + `;`
   to enter current time.

3. Press .... `Enter`

   OR

   Click .... ☑

Insert Current Date or Time (Recalculating)

Inserts the current date or time, which will change to show the current date or time each time you recalculate the spreadsheet.

1. Select cell where date or time is to appear.

2. Type...=*now()*

3. Press .... `Enter`

    OR

    Click.. ☑

To format the cell with the desired date or time format to replace serial number; see p. 106.

Use Date or Time in Formula

Dates and times in cells may be referenced by standard cell references, for example, A12. To use an actual date or time in a formula, enclose it in single quotation marks, for example, '7/23/56.'

ENTER NUMBER OR DATE SERIES

1. Select cell containing number or date to start series.

2. Click and drag from starting to ending cell to select area.

3. Click **E**dit menu.. `Alt` + `E`

4. Click **Fi**ll Series.. `I`

5. Choose one of the following options:

    • **N**umber.. `N`

    • **D**ay.. `D`

    • **W**eekday.. `W`

(continued...)

ENTER NUMBER OR DATE SERIES (continued)

- <u>M</u>onth .... `M`

- <u>Y</u>ear .... `Y`

*NOTE: Day, Weekday, Month, and Year options are only
available if the starting cell is formatted as a date.*

6. Click <u>S</u>tep By .... `S`

7. Type desired series increment ....*number*

8. Click **OK**... `Enter`

FORMAT CELLS

Change Cell Alignment

*Works automatically left-aligns cells containing text and right-aligns
cells containing formulas.*

Toolbar

1. Select cells to change.

2. Click... [icon]
    to left-align cells.

    OR

    Click.. [icon]
    to right-align cells.

    OR

    Click .... [icon]
    to center cells.

(continued...)

110

Shortcut Keys

1. Select cells to change.

2. Press.. `Ctrl` + `L`
   to left-align cells.

   OR

   Press.. `Ctrl` + `R`
   to right-align cells.

   OR

   Press.. `Ctrl` + `E`
   to center cells.

Wrap Text Inside Cell

1. Select cell(s) to change.

2. Click **Format** menu .... `Alt` + `T`

3. Click **Alignment**.. `A`

4. Click **Wrap Text**.. `W`

5. Click **OK**.. `Enter`

Center Text or Number over Columns

1. Select columns over which to center text or number.

   *NOTE: Any text or numbers that are longer than the
   column widths will be entirely displayed.*

2. Click **Format** menu .... `Alt` + `T`

3. Click **Alignment**.. `A`

4. Click **Center Across Selection** .... `A`

5. Click **OK**.. `Enter`

Change Vertical Alignment of Cell Contents

1. Select cell(s) to change.

2. Click **Format** menu .... `Alt` + `T`

3. Click **Alignment** .... `A`

4. Choose one of the following options:

   • **Top** .... `T`

   • **Center** .... `E`

   • **Bottom** .... `B`

5. Click **OK** .... `Enter`

CHANGE FONTS

Toolbar

1. Select cells to change.

2. Click list button .... `↓`
   to right of current font name.

3. Select desired font .... `↓`

4. Press .... `Enter`

5. Click size button .... `↓`
   to right of current font size.

6. Select size .... `↓`

7. Click **OK** .... `Enter`

112

Change Color

1. Select cells to change.
2. Click **Format** menu .... `Alt` + `T`
3. Click **Font & Style** .... `F`
4. Click **Color** .... `Alt` + `O`
5. Choose desired color .... `↓`
6. Click **OK** .... `Enter`

Change Font, Size and Color Simultaneously

1. Select cells to change.
2. Click **Format** menu .... `Alt` + `T`
3. Click **Font & Style** .... `F`
4. Click **Font** .... `Alt` + `F`
5. Select desired font .... `↓`
6. Click **Size** .... `Alt` + `S`
7. Select desired size .... `↓`
8. Click **Color** .... `Alt` + `O`
9. Select desired color .... `↓`
10. Click **OK** .... `Enter`

Underline

1. Select cells to underline.

(continued...)

UNDERLINE (continued)

2. Click.. $\boxed{\underline{\mathbf{u}}}$

   OR

   Press.. $\boxed{\text{Ctrl}}$ + $\boxed{\text{U}}$

Bold

1. Select cells to make bold.

2. Click.. $\boxed{\mathbf{B}}$

   OR

   Press.. $\boxed{\text{Ctrl}}$ + $\boxed{\text{B}}$

Italics

1. Select cells to italicize.

2. Click.. $\boxed{\mathit{I}}$

   OR

   Press.. $\boxed{\text{Ctrl}}$ + $\boxed{\text{I}}$

Return to Plain Text

1. Select cells to make plain.

2. Press.. $\boxed{\text{Ctrl}}$ + $\boxed{\text{S}}$

Change Cell Borders

1. Select cells to format with borders.

2. Click **Format** menu .... $\boxed{\text{Alt}}$ + $\boxed{\text{T}}$

(continued...)

CHANGE CELL BORDERS (continued)

3. Click **B**order.. `B`

4. Choose border to change from the following options:

   • **O**utline...................................... `Alt` + `O`

   • **T**op.. `Alt` + `T`

   • Botto**m** .... `Alt` + `M`

   • **L**eft.. `Alt` + `L`

   • **R**ight .... `Alt` + `R`

5. Choose desired **Line Style** .... `Alt` + `I` , `↓`

   NOTE: The top line style option will remove the border.

6. Choose desired **C**olor.......................... `Alt` + `C` , `↓`

7 Repeat steps 4 to 6 to change additional borders.

8. Click **OK**.. `Enter`

Shade Cells

1. Select cells to shade.

2. Click **Forma t** .... `Alt` + `T`

3. Click **P**atterns.................................... `P`

4. Select desired pattern.............................. `↓`

5. Click **F**oreground text box .... `Alt` + `F`

6. Select color.. `↓`

   NOTE: Choose Auto for no color

(continued...)

SHADE CELLS (continued)

7   Click **B**ackground text box.............................. `Alt` + `B`

8   Select color.. `↓`

    NOTE: *Choose Auto for no color.*

9.   Click **OK**.. `Enter`

AUTOFORMAT

Quickly changes a spreadsheet's lettering, borders and other formatting features to any of a number of professionally designed styles.

1.   Select cells to format.

2.   Click **Forma**t menu .... `Alt` + `T`

3.   Click **Autofor**m**at** .... `M`

4.   Choose **T**able **Format** from list box.............................. `↓`

Examples will appear.

5.   Click **OK**.. `Enter`

FORMAT NUMBERS AND DATA

1.   Select cells to format.

2.   Click **Forma**t menu .... `Alt` + `T`

3.   Click **N**umber .... `N`

(continued...)

FORMAT NUMBERS AND DATA (continued)

4. Choose desired format from the following options:

   • <u>G</u>eneral .... `G`

   • Fi<u>x</u>ed .... `X`

   • C<u>u</u>rrency .... `U`

   • <u>C</u>omma. .... `C`

   • <u>P</u>ercent .... `P`

   • <u>E</u>xponential .... `E`

   • <u>L</u>eading Zeros .... `L`

   • Fr<u>a</u>ction .... `A`

   • True/<u>F</u>alse .... `F`

   • <u>D</u>ate .... `D`

   • T<u>i</u>me .... `I`

   • <u>T</u>ext .... `T`

5. Type desired number ....*number*
   of decimals.

6. Click **OK** .... `Enter`

Change Standard Number of Decimal Places

1. Click **T<u>oo</u>ls** menu .... `Alt` + `O`

2. Click **<u>O</u>ptions** .... `O`

3. Click **Default Num<u>b</u>er of Decimals** .... `B`

(continued...)

CHANGE STANDARD NUMBER OF DECIMAL PLACES (continued)

4. Type desired number ....*number* of default decimals.

5. Click **OK**.. | Enter |

Format Numbers as Currency

1. Select cells to format.

2. Click.. | $ |

FORMAT PAGES

Insert Page Break

Works will automatically start new pages when necessary. To start a new page before the previous page is full, insert a page break.

1. Select row, column or cell where page is to horizontally or vertically break.

2. Click **I**nsert menu.................................... | Alt | + | I |

3. Click **Page Break**...................................... | B |

4. Choose desired location from the following options:

    • **R**ow .... | R |

    • **C**olumn.. | C |

5. Click **OK**.. | Enter |

Delete Page Break

Only a manual page break (one that you have previously set) can be deleted.

1. Select row below or column to right of page break to delete.

(continued...)

DELETE PAGE BREAK (continued)

2. Click **I**nsert menu.. `Alt` + `I`

3. Click **Delete Page Break**... `G`

FORMAT COLUMNS AND ROWS

Change Column Width or Row Height

Click and drag column border (vertical line between column labels) or row border (horizontal line between row labels) to desired size.

Set Precise Column or Row Size

1. Select any cells in columns or rows to change.

2. Click **Forma**t menu .... `Alt` + `T`

3. Click **Column** **W**idth .... `W`

    OR

    Click **Row** **H**eight .... `H`

4. Type a number between 0 and 79.............................*number*

5. Click **OK**... `Enter`

Resize Column or Row to Fit Largest Entry Automatically

Double-click row number or column label.

OR

1. Select columns or rows to change.

2. Click **Forma**t menu .... `Alt` + `T`

(continued...)

**RESIZE COLUMN OR ROW TO FIT LARGEST ENTRY
AUTOMATICALLY (continued)**

3. Click **Column Width** .... `W`

    OR

    Click **Row Height** .... `H`

4. Click **Best Fit** to select (☒).

5. Click **OK** .... `Enter`

Insert Rows or Columns

1. Select entire rows or columns where new rows or columns
    are to appear.

2. Click **Insert** menu .... `Alt` + `I`

3. Click **Row/Column** .... `R`

Delete Rows or Columns

1. Select cells in rows or columns to delete.

2. Click **Insert** menu .... `Alt` + `I`

3. Click **Delete Row/Column** .... `D`

4. Choose one of the following options:

    • **Rows** .... `R`

    • **Columns** .... `C`

5. Click **OK** .... `Enter`

120

Hide a Column or Row

> *NOTE:* *Hidden columns and rows do not appear in the spreadsheet window and do not print, but may be used in calculations. Protected columns cannot be hidden until protection is turned off.*

Click and drag right column border (to right of column label) to left until it meets left column border.

OR

Click and drag bottom row border (below row number) up until it meets top row border.

Hide Several Columns or Rows

1. Select a cell from each column or row to hide.

2. Click **Format** menu .... |Alt| + |T|

3. Click **Column Width** .... |W|

   OR

   Click **Row Height** .... |H|

4. Press .... |O|

5. Click **OK** .... |Enter|

Display Hidden Column

1. Click **Edit** menu .... |Alt| + |E|

2. Click **Go to** .... |G|

3. Type cell address .... *cell address*
   in column to display.

4. Click **OK** .... |Enter|

(continued...)

DISPLAY HIDDEN COLUMN (continued)

5. Click **Forma_t** menu .... `Alt` + `T`

6. Click **W_idth:** .... `Alt` + `W`

7. Type number ....*number*
   for new width for column.

8. Click **OK** .... `Enter`

Print Row and Column Headings

1. Click **F_ile** menu .... `Alt` + `F`

2. Click **Pa_ge Setup** .... `G`

3. Click **O_ther Options** tab .... `Alt` + `O`

4. Click **Print ro_w and column headers** .... `Alt` + `W`
   to select (☒).

5. Click **OK** .... `Enter`

SEARCH FOR MATCHING TEXT OR VALUES

1. Select cells to search.

   NOTE: Search entire spreadsheet, do not select any cells.

2. Click **E_dit** menu .... `Alt` + `E`

3. Click **F_ind** .... `F`

4. Type text or number to find ....*text*

(continued...)

SEARCH FOR MATCHING TEXT OR VALUES (continued)

5. Choose one of the following **Look By** order options:

- Rows .... `Alt` + `R`
  to search from left to right.

   OR

- Columns .... `Alt` + `C`
  to search from top to bottom.

6. Choose one of the following **Look In** order options:

- Formulas .... `Alt` + `F`

- Values .... `Alt` + `V`

7. Click **OK** .... `Enter`

Repeat Previous Search

Press .... `F7`

SEARCH AND REPLACE MATCHING TEXT OR VALUES

1. Select cells to search.

   NOTE: Search entire spreadsheet, do not select any cells.

2. Click **Edit** menu .... `Alt` + `E`

3. Click **Replace** .... `R`

4. Type text or number to find.

5. Type replacement characters .... *text*

(continued...)

SEARCH AND REPLACE MATCHING TEXT OR VALUES (continued)

6. Choose one of the following **Look By** order options:

- R_o_ws .... `Alt` + `O`
  to search from left to right.

  OR

- _C_olumns .... `Alt` + `C`
  to search from top to bottom.

7. Click **_F_ind Next** .... `Alt` + `F`

8. Click **_R_eplace** .... `Alt` + `R`
   to replace and find next when matching
   characters are found.

   OR

   Click **_F_ind Next** .... `Alt` + `F`
   to continue without replacing.

   OR

   Click **Replace _A_ll** .... `Alt` + `A`
   to replace all occurrences automatically.

9. Click **Clos_e_** .... `Alt` + `E`
   when finished.

SORT DATA

Works sorts entries in cells alphabetically or numerically by entire rows. One to three columns may be chosen and prioritized for the sort. Mixed data types are sorted in the following order (ascending): text, times, numbers, dates. Blank cells are found at the end of either an ascending or descending sort.

1 Select rows to sort.

(continued...)

SORT DATA (continued)

2. Click **To͟ols** menu .... `Alt` + `O`

3. Click **So͟rt Records** .... `R`

4. Click **1͟st Column** .... `Alt` + `1`

5. Type letter ....*letter*
   of first priority column to sort.

6. Choose one of the following options:

   • Ascend **A͟** .... `Alt` + `A`

   • Descend **B͟** .... `Alt` + `B`

7. Repeat steps 4 to 6 for second and third priority columns,
   if desired.

8. Click **OK** .... `Enter`

CHOOSE MANUAL CALCULATION

*Works automatically calculates and recalculates data. If many
changes to a spreadsheet are being made, Works may be set to
Manual Calculation, under which it will only recalculate when
prompted.*

1. Click **To͟ols** menu .... `Alt` + `O`

2. Click **M͟anual Calculation** .... `M`

Calculate Manually

1. Click **To͟ols** menu .... `Alt` + `O`

2. Click **Calculate N͟ow** .... `N`

   OR

   Press .... `F9`

LOCK CELL CONTENTS

Protects cell contents from accidental changes. The Works default setting locks all cells, but until protection is turned on, the locks are not in effect.

1. Select cells to lock.

2. Click **Format** menu .... `Alt` + `T`

3. Click **Protection** .... `R`

4. Click **Locked** .... `L`

5. Click **OK** .... `Enter`

Turn Cell Protection On or Off

1. Select cells to be protected or unprotected.

2. Click **Format** menu .... `Alt` + `T`

3. Click **Protection** .... `R`

4. Click **Protect Data** .... `P`

5. Click **OK** .... `Enter`

USE SPREADSHEET WITH OTHER APPLICATIONS

Lets you use Works spreadsheets with Excel, Lotus 1-2-3 and other spreadsheet programs.

Open Spreadsheet from Another Application

1. Click **File** menu .... `Alt` + `F`

2. Click **Open Existing File** .... `O`

(continued...)

OPEN SPREADSHEET FROM ANOTHER APPLICATION (continued)

3. Click **List Files of Type**..............................`Alt` + `T`

4. Click desired file type ....`↓`

5. Click **File Name**....................................`Alt` + `N`

6. Type filename ....*filename*
   or choose filename from list.

7. Click **OK**..`Enter`

8. Click **Spreadsheet**.....................................`S`
   if necessary.

9. Click **OK**..`Enter`

Save Spreadsheet to Be Opened in Another Application

1. View spreadsheet to save.

2. Click **File** menu....................................`Alt` + `F`

3. Click **Save As** ....`A`

4. Click **Save File as Type**........................`Alt` + `T`

5. Choose desired file type from the following options:

   - Text & Commas

   - Text & Tabs

   - Text & Tabs (DOS)

   - Lotus 1-2-3

(continued...)

SAVE SPREADSHEET TO BE OPENED IN ANOTHER APPLICATION (continued)

- Excel 4.0/5.0SS

- Works Mac 3.0 ss

6. Click **File Name**.. `Alt` + `N`

7. Type new filename. ....*filename*
   If new filename is not chosen,
   original file will be replaced.

8. Click **OK**.. `Enter`

CREATE A CHART

Charts may be created from data in Works spreadsheets. Each spreadsheet supports up to eight charts. When spreadsheet data is updated, charts reflect the update.

– IN SPREADSHEET WINDOW –

1. Select cells that contain desired values and labels.

2. Click .... 🔣

   OR

   a. Click **Tools** menu .... `Alt` + `O`

   b. Click **Create New Chart**........................ `C`

– IN WHAT TYPE LIST BOX –

3. Choose desired type...................................... `↓`

(continued...)

128

CREATE A CHART (continued)

4. Add finishing touches, if desired:

- Click **Chart Title** text box .... `Alt` + `T`

  Type title ....*title*

  - Click **Add Borders** .... `Alt` + `B`

  - Click **Add Gridlines** .... `Alt` + `G`

  Choose desired series direction from the following options:

  - **A**cross .... `Alt` + `A`

  - **D**own .... `Alt` + `D`

6. Indicate first row contents (if text) by clicking desired option:

  - **L**egend texts .... `Alt` + `L`

  - A catego**r**y .... `Alt` + `R`

7. Indicate first column contents (if text) by clicking desired option:

  - **C**ategory labels .... `Alt` + `C`

  - A value of (**Y**) series .... `Alt` + `Y`

8. Check example at right.

9. Click **OK** .... `Enter`

THE CHART WINDOW AND TOOLBAR

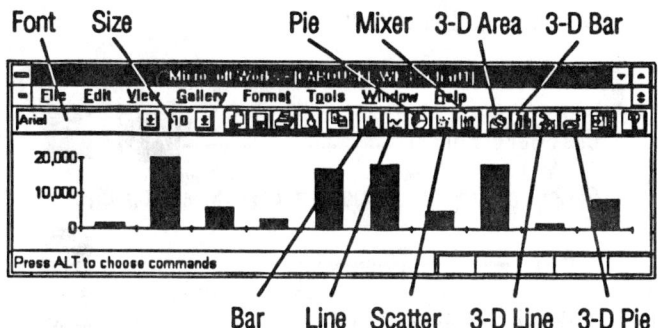

Font   Size   Pie   Mixer   3-D Area   3-D Bar

Bar   Line   Scatter   3-D Line   3-D Pie

SWITCH FROM CHART TO SPREADSHEET WINDOW

1. Click **View** menu .... `Alt` + `V`

2. Click **Spreadsheet** .... `S`

OR

1. Click **Window** menu .... `Alt` + `W`

2. Choose desired window to view.

VIEW CHART

1. Click **View** menu .... `Alt` + `V`

2. Click **Chart** .... `C`

3. Choose desired chart name .... `↓`

4. Click **OK** .... `Enter`

(continued...)

CHANGE CHART TYPE

1. View chart to change.

2. Click button for desired chart type.

   OR

   a. Click **Gallery** menu .... `Alt` + `G`

   b. Choose desired chart type from the following options:

   - <u>A</u>rea.. `A`
   - <u>B</u>ar .... `B`
   - <u>L</u>ine .... `L`
   - <u>P</u>ie .... `P`
   - <u>S</u>tacked .... `S`
   - <u>X</u>Y (scatter)... `X`
   - Ra<u>d</u>ar .... `D`
   - Co<u>m</u>bination .... `M`
   - 3-D <u>A</u>rea.. `A`
   - 3-D <u>B</u>ar .... `B`
   - 3-D <u>L</u>ine .... `L`
   - 3-D P<u>i</u>e .... `I`

3. Choose desired chart style .... `↓`

   OR

   Type number ....*number*
   for desired chart option.

   OR

(continued...)

CHANGE CHART TYPE (continued)

Click **Next** .... `N`
to see next chart type.

OR

Click **Previous** .... `P`
to see previous chart type.

4. Click **OK**.. `Enter`

Make Any Chart 3-D

1. View chart to change.

2. Click **Format** menu .... `Alt` + `T`

3. Click **Make 3-D**.. `3`

CHART MANAGEMENT

Save Chart

Works automatically saves charts with their associated spreadsheets.

Change Chart Name

1. Click **Tools** menu.................................... `Alt` + `O`

2. Click **Name Chart**....................................... `A`

3. Click **Name** .... `Alt` + `N`

4. Type desired name.

5. Click **Rename** .... `Alt` + `R`

6. Click **OK**.. `Enter`

Delete Chart

1. Click **Tools** menu .... Alt + O

2. Click **Delete Chart** I

3. Select chart .... ↓
   to delete.

4. Click **Delete** .... Alt + D

5. Click **OK** .... Enter

Duplicate Chart

1. Click **Tools** menu .... O

2. Click **Duplicate** I

3. Select chart .... ↓
   to duplicate.

4. Click **Duplicate** .... Alt + U

Chart is automatically named.

5. Click **OK** .... Enter

EDIT CHART

Create Chart from Non-Adjacent Cells

– IN SPREADSHEET WINDOW –

1. Select adjacent cells (if any) to include in chart.

(continued...)

CREATE CHART FROM NON-ADJACENT CELLS (continued)

– ON TOOLBAR –

2. Click **Chart** button .... 📊

   OR

   a. Click **Tools** menu .... `Alt` + `O`

   b. Click **Create New Chart** .... `C`

3. Choose chart options, as desired.

4. Click **Edit** menu .... `Alt` + `E`

5. Click **Series** .... `S`

6. Click first empty series box:

   • 1st .... `Alt` + `1`

   • 2nd .... `Alt` + `2`

   • 3rd .... `Alt` + `3`

   • 4th .... `Alt` + `4`

   • 5th .... `Alt` + `5`

   • 6th .... `Alt` + `6`

   • Category (X) Series .... `Alt` + `C`

7. Type cell reference for series .... *cell reference*
   (see page 103).

8. Repeat steps 6 and 7 for each new series to add.

9. Click **OK** .... `Enter`

Find Cells Used in Chart

1. View chart used to locate cells.

2. Press .... `F5`

   OR

   a. Click **E**dit menu .... `Alt` + `E`

   b. Click **G**o to .... `G`

3. Choose desired series to select (◉):

   - **1**st .... `1`

   - **2**nd .... `2`

   - **3**rd .... `3`

   - **4**th .... `4`

   - **5**th .... `5`

   - **6**th .... `6`

   - **C**ategory .... `C`

4. Click **OK** .... `Enter`

Add or Change Series of Values in Chart

1. View spreadsheet with cells to add.

2. Select cells.

3. Click .... 📋

   OR

   a. Click **E**dit menu .... `Alt` + `E`

(continued...)

ADD OR CHANGE SERIES OF VALUES IN CHART (continued)

    b. Click **C**opy .... `C`

4. Click **W**indow menu .... `Alt`

5. Select chart to change .... `W`

6. Click **E**dit menu .... `Alt` + `E`

7. Click **P**aste Series .... `P`

8. Click desired series to select (◉):

    • **1**st .... `1`

    • **2**nd .... `2`

    • **3**rd .... `3`

    • **4**th .... `4`

    • **5**th .... `5`

    • **6**th .... `6`

    • **C**ategory .... `C`

9. Click OK .... `Enter`

Delete Series of Values

1. View chart with values to delete.

2. Click **E**dit menu .... `Alt` + `E`

3. Click **S**eries .... `S`

4. Select range reference for series to delete.

(continued...)

DELETE SERIES OF VALUES (continued)

5. Press .... `Del`

6. Click **OK**.. `Enter`

FORMAT CHART

Scale Axis

> *NOTE:* *An axis is the vertical or horizontal line beside or below a chart to indicate increments of value. In bar and line charts, the vertical (Y) axis may be changed in scale. In XY charts, only the horizontal axis may be scaled.*

1. View chart to change.

2. Click **Format** menu .... `Alt` + `T`

3. Choose one of the following axes to change:

   - Horizontal (X) Axis .... `H`

   - Vertical (Y) Axis.................................... `V`

   - Right Vertical Axis .... `R`

   - Two Vertical (X) Axes .... `T`

4. Click **Minimum:**................................... `Alt` + `M`

5. Type new minimum value ....*value*
   to show on chart.

6. Click **Maximum** .... `Alt` + `X`

7. Type new maximum value ....*value*
   to show on chart.

(continued...)

SCALE AXIS (continued)

8. Click **Interval**... `Alt` + `I`

9. Type new interval value ....*value*
between axis marks.

10. Click **Use Logarithmic Scale** .... `Alt` + `L`

11 Click **OK**.. `Enter`

Add Right Vertical Axis

> *NOTE:* *Two series of numbers must be used to display a*
> *right vertical axis.*

1 Click **Format** menu .... `Alt` + `T`

2. Click **Two Vertical (Y) Axes** .... `T`

3. Choose from the following **Right** option
buttons for desired value series to add (◉):

- 1st Value Series - Right **B** .... `B`

- 2nd Value Series - Right **D** .... `D`

- 3rd Value Series - Right **F** .... `F`

- 4th Value Series - Right **I** .... `I`

- 5th Value Series - Right **K** .... `K`

- 6th Value Series - Right **M** .... `M`

4. Click **OK**.. `Enter`

Remove Right Vertical Axis

1. Click **Format** menu .... `Alt` + `T`

2. Click **Right Vertical Axis**................................... `R`

3. Click **No Vertical Axis** .... `A`

Combine Chart Types with Right Vertical Axis

1. View chart to change.

2. Click **Format** menu .... `Alt` + `T`

3. Choose axis to change:

   • **Vertical (Y) Axis**..................................... `V`

   • **Right Vertical Axis** .... `R`

4. Choose one of the following options:

   • **Normal** .... `Alt` + `N`

   • **Stacked** .... `Alt` + `S`

   • **100%** .... `Alt` + `1`

   • **Hi-Lo** .... `Alt` + `H`

5. Click **OK**.. `Enter`

Add or Remove Horizontal Axis

1. Click **Format** menu .... `Alt` + `T`

2. Click **Horizontal Axis**..................................... `H`

3. Click **No Horizontal Axis** .... `A`

Add or Remove Vertical Axis

1. Click **Format** menu .... `Alt` + `T`

2. Click **Vertical Axis** .... `V`

3. Click **No Vertical Axis** .... `A`

Explode Pie Slice

Pulls a segment of a pie chart away from the center for emphasis.

1. View pie chart to change.

2. Click **Format** menu .... `Alt` + `T`

3. Click **Patterns & Colors** .... `P`

4. Select **Slices** .... `Alt` + `S`

5. Select slice to explode .... `↓`

6. Click **Explode Slice** .... `Alt` + `E`

7. Click **Format** .... `Alt` + `F`

   OR

   Click **Format All** .... `Alt` + `A`
   to explode all slices.

8. Click **Close** .... `Alt` + `C`

Mix Lines and Bars in Chart

> *NOTE:* *Chart must have at least two series of numbers to include both lines and bars. Pie charts do not support mixed lines and bars.*

1. View chart to change.

(continued...)

MIX LINES AND BARS IN CHART (continued)

2. Click **Format** menu .... `Alt` + `T`

3. Click **Mixed Line & Bar** .... `M`

4. Choose one of the following **1st Value (Y)** Series options:

   - Line **A** .... `A`

   - Bar **B** .... `B`

5. Choose one of the following **2nd Value (Y)** Series options:

   - Line **C** .... `C`

   - Bar **D** .... `D`

6. Choose one of the following **3rd Value (Y)** Series option to select ({{):

   - Line **E** .... `E`

   - Bar **F** .... `F`

7. Choose one of the following **4th Value (Y)** Series options:

   - Line **G** .... `G`

   - Bar **I** .... `I`

8. Choose one of the following **5th Value (Y)** Series options:

   - Line **J** .... `J`

   - Bar **K** .... `K`

9. Choose one of the following **6th Value (Y)** Series options:

(continued...)

MIX LINES AND BARS IN CHART (continued)

- Line <u>L</u>... `L`

- Bar <u>M</u>... `M`

10. Click **OK**... `Enter`

Add or Remove Gridlines to Chart

1. View chart to change.

2. Click **Forma<u>t</u>** menu .... `Alt` + `T`

3. Click axis to which to add gridlines:

   - <u>H</u>orizontal (X) Axis .... `H`

   - <u>V</u>ertical (Y) Axis .... `V`

   - <u>R</u>ight Vertical (Y) Axis .... `R`

4. Click **Show <u>G</u>ridlines** .... `G`

5. Click **OK**.. `Enter`

Add or Remove Border

1. View chart to change.

2. Click **Forma<u>t</u>** menu .... `Alt` + `T`

3. Click **Add <u>B</u>order** .... `B`

Change Chart Marker Shapes

> *NOTE: Marker shapes may not be changed on pie or bar charts.*

1. View chart to change.

(continued...)

CHANGE CHART MARKER SHAPES (continued)

2. Click **Forma_t_** menu .... `Alt` + `T`

3. Click **_P_atterns & Colors** .... `P`

4. Choose series to change from the following options:

   • _1_st .... `Alt` + `1`

   • _2_nd .... `Alt` + `2`

   • _3_rd .... `Alt` + `3`

   • _4_th .... `Alt` + `4`

   • _5_th .... `Alt` + `5`

   • _6_th .... `Alt` + `6`

5. Click **_M_arkers** .... `Alt` + `M`

6. Select desired marker type .... `↓`

7. Click **_F_ormat** .... `Alt` + `F`

   OR

   Click **Format _A_ll** .... `Alt` + `A`

8. Repeat steps 4-7 for each series to change.

9. Click **_C_lose** .... `Alt` + `C`

ADD OR REMOVE DROPLINES

Droplines can only be added to an area chart.

1. View chart to change.

(continued...)

ADD OR REMOVE DROPLINES (continued)

2. Click **Format** menu .... `Alt` + `T`

3. Click **Horizontal Axis** .... `H`

4. Click **Show Droplines** .... `Alt` + `D`

EDIT CHART TEXT

Add or Edit Chart Titles

1. View chart to which you would like to add or edit title.

2. Click **Edit** menu .... `Alt` + `E`

3. Click **Titles** .... `T`

4. Choose one of the following title boxes to add or change:

   - **Chart title:** .... `Alt` + `C`

   - **Subtitle:** .... `Alt` + `S`

   - **Horizontal (X) Axis:** .... `Alt` + `O`

   - **Vertical (Y) Axis:** .... `Alt` + `V`

   - **Right Vertical Axis:** .... `Alt` + `R`

5. Type title or range reference title or range reference.
   for cell containing title text.

   OR

   Type text ....*text*
   in text box.

   OR

(continued...)

ADD OR EDIT CHART TITLES (continued)

Paste reference from clipboard.

NOTE: *Reference must first be copied to clipboard from spreadsheet.*

6. Click **OK**.. `Enter`

Delete Chart Titles

1. View chart with titles to delete.

2. Click **E**dit menu... `Alt` + `E`

3. Click **T**itles.. `T`

4. Choose from the following title boxes:

   • **C**hart title:.. `Alt` + `C`

   • **S**ubtitle:... `Alt` + `S`

   • H**o**rizontal (X) Axis:.................................. `Alt` + `O`

   • **V**ertical (Y) Axis: .... `Alt` + `V`

   • **R**ight Vertical Axis:.................................. `Alt` + `R`

5. Select text or range reference to delete.

6. Press .... `Del`

7. Click **OK**.. `Enter`

Add or Edit Category Labels

1. Enter category labels in spreadsheet cells.

2. Select cells for labels.

(continued...)

ADD OR EDIT CATEGORY LABELS (continued)

3. Click .... 🖺

    OR

    a. Click **E**dit menu .... Alt + E

    b. Click **C**opy C

4. Click **W**indow menu .... Alt + W

5. Choose chart to change.

6. Click **E**dit menu .... Alt + E

7. Click **P**aste Series .... Alt + P

8. Click **C**ategory C

9. Click **L**abels L

10. Click **OK** .... Enter

Remove Category Labels

1. View chart to change.

2. Click **E**dit menu .... Alt + E

3. Click **D**ata Labels .... D

4. Select range reference from series labels to delete.

5. Press .... Del

6. Click **OK** .... Enter

Change Category Label Frequency

1. View chart to change.

2. Click **Format** menu .... `Alt` + `T`

3. Click **Horizontal (X) Axis** .... `H`

4. Click **Label Frequency:** .... `Alt` + `L`

5. Type number ....*number*
   for points between labels.

6. Click **OK** .... `Enter`

Add Data Labels to Pie Chart

1. View pie chart to change.

2. Click **Edit** menu .... `Alt` + `E`

3. Click **Data Labels** .... `D`

4. Click option to select (◉) for first label, if desired:

   • **Values** .... `Alt` + `V`

   • **Percentages** .... `Alt` + `E`

   • **Cell Contents** .... `Alt` + `C`

      a. Click **Cell Range** .... `Alt` + `R`

      b. Type range to use ....*range*

   • **1**, 2, 3, ... `Alt` + `1`

   • **None** .... `Alt` + `N`

5. Click an option to select (◉) for second label, if desired:

   • **Values** .... `Alt` + `V`

(continued...)

ADD DATA LABELS TO PIE CHART (continued)

- Percentages .... `Alt` + `E`
- Cell Contents .... `Alt` + `C`

   a. Click **Cell Range** .... `Alt` + `R`

   b. Type range to use.................................*range*

- 1, 2, 3,.. `Alt` + `1`
- None.. `Alt` + `N`

6. Click **OK**.. `Enter`

Remove Data Labels on Pie Chart

1. View pie chart to change.

2. Click **Edit** menu................................ `Alt` + `E`

3. Click **Data Labels**................................... `D`

   To remove first labels:

   Click **None** .... `N`

   To remove second labels:

   Click **None**................................... `Alt` + `O`

4. Click **OK**.. `Enter`

Use Cell Contents as Data Labels in Line or Bar Chart

1. Add text or values for labels to spreadsheet.

(continued...)

148

USE CELL CONTENTS AS DATA LABELS IN LINE OR BAR CHART (continued)

2   Select cells for labels.

- ON TOOLBAR -

3. Click.. 📑

    OR

    a. Click **E**dit menu... `Alt` + `E`

    b. Click **C**opy.. `C`

4. Click **W**indow menu .... `Alt`

5. Choose chart to open .... `W`

6. Click **E**dit menu .... `Alt` + `E`

7. Click **D**ata Labels... `D`

8. Choose one of the following Value (Y) Series:

    • **1**st.. `Alt` + `1`

    • **2**nd.. `Alt` + `2`

    • **3**rd... `Alt` + `3`

    • **4**th.. `Alt` + `4`

    • **5**th.. `Alt` + `5`

    • **6**th.. `Alt` + `6`

Make sure the Use Series Values checkbox is clear.

9. Click **P**aste.. `Alt` + `P`

10. Click **OK**... `Enter`

Use Bar or Line Chart's Plotted Values as Labels

1. View chart to change.

2. Click **E**dit menu.. `Alt` + `E`

3. Click **D**ata Labels... `D`

4. Click **U**se series data .... `Alt` + `U`
   to select (☒).

5. Click **OK**... `Enter`

Remove Data Labels from Line or Bar Charts

1. View chart to change.

2. Click **E**dit menu.. `Alt` + `E`

3. Click **D**ata Labels... `D`

4. Choose one of the following **Value (Y)** Series boxes to remove:

   - **1**st.. `Alt` + `1`

   - **2**nd... `Alt` + `2`

   - **3**rd.. `Alt` + `3`

   - **4**th.. `Alt` + `4`

   - **5**th.. `Alt` + `5`

   - **6**th.. `Alt` + `6`

   - **U**se series data .... `Alt` + `U`
     to deselect (☐).

5. Select cell reference.

(continued...)

REMOVING DATA LABELS FROM LINE OR BAR CHARTS (continued)

6. Press .... `Del`

7. Click **OK** .... `Enter`

Add or Edit Legend Marker

NOTE: *Works automatically creates a legend for each chart. If you haven't included legend text in your spreadsheet, Works uses Series 1, Series 2, etc. as legend text.*

1. Enter text for legend in spreadsheet cells, if desired.

2. Click **W**indow menu .... `Alt` + `W`

3. Choose chart to change.

4. Click **E**dit menu .... `Alt` + `E`

5. Click **Legend/Series Labels** .... `L`

6. Choose one of the following value series to change:

   • **1**st Value Series .... `Alt` + `1`

   • **2**nd Value Series .... `Alt` + `2`

   • **3**rd Value Series .... `Alt` + `3`

   • **4**th Value Series .... `Alt` + `4`

   • **5**th Value Series .... `Alt` + `5`

   • **6**th Value Series .... `Alt` + `6`

7. Type cell reference or legend ....*text* up to 19 characters long.

8. Click **OK** .... `Enter`

Remove Legend Marker

1. View chart to change.

2. Click **Edit** menu.. `Alt` + `E`

3. Click **Legend/Series Labels** .... `L`

4. Choose one of the following **Value Series** box options to remove:

   • **1**st Value Series .... `Alt` + `1`

   • **2**nd Value Series .... `Alt` + `2`

   • **3**rd Value Series.. `Alt` + `3`

   • **4**th Value Series .... `Alt` + `4`

   • **5**th Value Series .... `Alt` + `5`

   • **6**th Value Series .... `Alt` + `6`

5. Select range reference or text.

6. Press .... `Del`

7. Repeat steps 4 to 6 for each marker to remove.

8. Click **OK**.. `Enter`

View or Hide Legends

1. Click **Format** menu .... `Alt` + `T`

2. Click **Add Legend** .... `L`
   to select (⦿) or clear.

FORMAT CHART TEXT

Change Chart Fonts, Font Styles, and Sizes

1. View chart to change.

   OR

   To change title only:

   Select chart title on chart.

2. Select desired font in font list box.

3. Select desired font size.

   OR

1. View chart to change.

   OR

   To change title only:

   Select chart title on chart.

2. Click **Format** menu .... `Alt` + `T`

3. Click **Font and Style** .... `F`

4. Click desired **Font** .... `Alt` + `F`, `↓`

5. Click desired **Size** .... `Alt` + `S`, `↓`

6. Choose desired font style from the following options:

   • **Bold** .... `B`

   • **Italic** .... `I`

   • **Underline** .... `U`

   • **Strikethrough** .... `T`

(continued...)

CHANGE CHART FONTS, FONT STYLES, AND SIZES (continued)

7. Click C**o**lor... `Alt` + `O`, `↓`

8. Click **OK**.. `Enter`

FORMAT CHART COLORS AND PATTERNS

Change Bar or Pie Chart Colors and Patterns

1. View chart to change.

2. Click **Forma**t menu .... `Alt` + `T`

3. Click **P**atterns and Colors............................ `P`

4. Click series to change from the following options:

   - **1**st... `Alt` + `1`

   - **2**nd.. `Alt` + `2`

   - **3**rd... `Alt` + `3`

   - **4**th... `Alt` + `4`

   - **5**th... `Alt` + `5`

   - **6**th... `Alt` + `6`

5. Click C**o**lors.. `Alt` + `O`

6. Select desired color............................... `↓`

7. Click **P**atterns .... `Alt` + `P`

8. Select desired patte**r**n.

(continued...)

CHANGE BAR OR PIE CHART COLORS AND PATTERNS (continued)

9. Click **Format** .... `Alt` + `F`
    to change selected series.

    OR

    Click **Format All** .... `Alt` + `A`
    to change all series.

10. Repeat steps 4-7 for each series to change.

11. Click **Close** .... `Alt` + `C`

Display Chart in Black and White

1. View chart to display.

2. Click **View** menu .... `Alt` + `V`

3   Click **Display As Printed** .... `P`
    to select (◉).

Database

THE DATABASE WINDOW

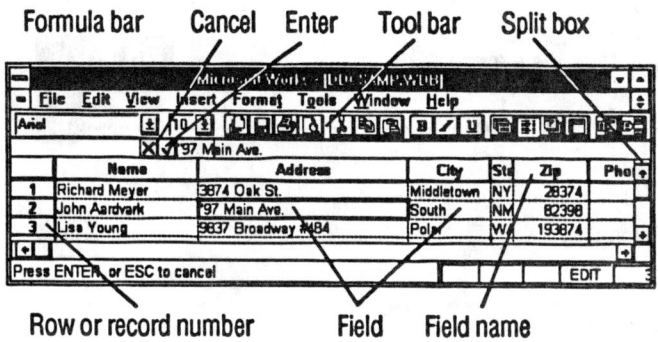

Formula bar   Cancel   Enter   Tool bar   Split box

Row or record number   Field   Field name

FORM VIEW

Form view displays one record of the database at a time.

– ON TOOLBAR –

Click .... 🗇

OR

1. Click **V**iew .... **Alt** + **V**

2. Click **F**orm .... **F**

OR

Press **F9**

(continued...)

LIST VIEW

List view displays multiple records of the database organized as a chart.

Click.. 🏢

OR

1. Click **V**iew menu.. `Alt` + `V`

2. Click **L**ist view .... `L`

OR

Press .... `F9`

CREATE FIELD

Create Field in Form View

> *NOTE: Each category of information in a database should have its own field. Each field must have a unique name.*

1. Place insertion point where field is to appear.

2. Type field name...*field name:*
   followed by a colon(:).

   > *NOTE: Field names may be up to 15 characters long. Single quotation marks (') may not begin field names.*

3. Press .... `↵`

4. Type number of characters ....*number*
   for field width.

5. Click **H**e**i**ght .... `Alt` + `E`

(continued...)

CREATE FIELD IN FORM VIEW (continued)

6. Type number of lines ....*number*
   for field height.

7. Click **OK**..↵

Create Field in List View

1. Click to select any field in empty column.

2. Click **Edit** menu........................... **Alt** + **E**

3. Click **Field Name** .... **N**

4. Type name ....*name*
   in text box.

5. Click **OK**..↵

ENTER INFORMATION IN FIELD

1. Click field to enter information.

2. Type information..................................*data*

   *NOTE: Press **Shift+Enter** to add text to the additional lines
   of a multi-line field.*

3. Press .... **Tab**
   to move to next field.

   OR

   Press............................... **Shift** + **Tab**
   to move to previous field.

   OR

   Press ....↵

ENTER FORMULA INTO FIELD

1. Click field to contain formula.

2. Type .... `=`

3. Type formula, using field names, mathematical symbols, and numbers and function (see appendix, p. 261).

   Subtraction .... `-`

   Addition .... `+`

   Multiplication.. `*`

   Division.. `/`

4. Press .... `↵`

*Example: =Qty * Unit price*

MOVE AROUND DATABASE

Scroll Through Database

Lets you view different parts of a database too large to fit on one screen. Scrolling does not move the insertion point.

Click scroll bar .... `↑` `↓`
until desired screen appears.

OR

Click and drag scroll bar slider until desired screen appears.

(continued...)

Scroll from Record to Record in Form View

First record .... ⏮

Previous record .... ⏴

Next record .... ⏵

Last record .... ⏭

> NOTE: The last record is always blank.

Move Through Form View Using Keystrokes

Next unlocked field .... `Tab`

Previous unlocked field .... `Shift` + `Tab`

Left side of form .... `Home`

Right side of form .... `End`

Down one screen .... `PgDn`

Up one screen .... `PgUp`

Left one screen .... `Ctrl` + `←`

Right one screen .... `Ctrl` + `→`

First record .... `Ctrl` + `Home`

Last record .... `Ctrl` + `End`

Next record .... `Ctrl` + `PgDn`

Previous record .... `Ctrl` + `PgUp`

Move Through List View Using Keystrokes

Left/right one field...⟨←⟩, ⟨→⟩

Up/down one field...⟨↑⟩, ⟨↓⟩

Next unlocked field...⟨Tab⟩

Previous unlocked field.............................⟨Shift⟩ + ⟨Tab⟩

First field at left...⟨Home⟩

Last field at right..⟨End⟩

Down one screen...⟨PgDn⟩

Up one screen...⟨PgUp⟩

Left one screen...⟨Ctrl⟩ + ⟨PgUp⟩

Right one screen.......................................⟨Ctrl⟩ + ⟨PgDn⟩

First field of first record........................⟨Ctrl⟩ + ⟨Home⟩

Last field of last record..........................⟨Ctrl⟩ + ⟨End⟩

SELECT OR HIGHLIGHT

Select Field Name Field Entry or Field Label in Form View

Click desired item

OR

Press tab and arrow keys .....⟨Tab⟩, ⟨↑⟩, ⟨↓⟩, ⟨←⟩, ⟨→⟩
until item is selected

Select More than One Element in Form View

1 Press and hold...⟨Ctrl⟩

2. Click desired elements.

Select Record in Form View

Click record arrow buttons until record appears:

- First record .... |◄|

- Previous record .... |◄|

- Next record .... |►|

- Last record .... |►|

OR

Press keystrokes until record appears:

- Previous record .... `Ctrl` + `PgUp`

- Next record .... `Ctrl` + `PgDn`

Select Field Entry in Form View

Click field entry.

OR

Press tab .... `Tab`
until field entry is highlighted.

Select Field Entry in List View

Click field entry.

OR

Press tab .... `Tab`
until field entry is highlighted.

OR

Press arrow keys .... `↑`, `↓`, `←`, `→`
until field is highlighted.

Select Several Entries in List View

Click and drag from one corner to opposite
corner of desired field entries.

OR

Press **Shift** and arrow keys ... `Shift` , `↑` , `↓` , `←` , `→`
until field is highlighted.

Select Record in List View

Click record number.

OR

a. Select any field from record.

b. Press..`Ctrl` + `F8`

Select All Entries in Field in List View

Click field name.

OR

a. Select field from any record.

b. Press..`Shift` + `F8`

Select Entire Database in List View

Click corner above top record number.

OR

Press ....`Ctrl` + `Shift` + `F8`

SHOW OR HIDE FIELD PERIMETERS IN FORM VIEW

1. Click **V**iew menu .... `Alt` + `V`

2. Click **Fi**eld Lines .... `I`
   to select (✓) or clear.

SHOW OR HIDE FIELD PERIMETERS IN LIST VIEW

1. Click **V**iew menu .... `Alt` + `V`

2. Click **G**ridlines .... `G`
   to select (✓) or clear.

EDIT FIELDS

Add and Name Field in List View

1. Select field to right of where new field is to appear.

2. Click **I**nsert menu .... `Alt` + `I`

3. Click **R**ecord/Field .... `R`

4. Click **F**ield .... `F`
   to select (◉).

5. Click **OK** .... `↵`

6. Click **E**dit menu .... `Alt` + `E`

7. Click Field **N**ame .... `N`

8. Type field name .... *field name*

   NOTE: *Field names may be up to 15 characters long, but*
   when single quotation marks (') may not begin field
   names.

9. Click **OK** .... `↵`

Delete Field in Form View

NOTE: Deleting a field deletes all its entries.

1.   Select field to delete.

2.   Click **I**nsert menu...................................... `Alt` + `I`

3.   Click **Delete S**election .... `S`

4.   Click **OK** to confirm deletion.. `↵`

Delete Field in List View

NOTE: Deleting a field deletes all its entries.

1.   Select field or fields to delete.

2.   Click **I**nsert menu...................................... `Alt` + `I`

3.   Click **D**elete Record/Field .... `D`

Delete Field Entry

1.   Select field or fields containing entries to delete.

2.   Click **E**dit menu.. `Alt` + `E`

3.   Click **Cl**ear Field Entry .... `E`

Clear Formula from Field

– IN FORM VIEW –

1.   Select field containing formula to clear.

   OR

– IN LIST VIEW –

   Select entire field column containing formula to clear.

(continued...)

CLEAR FORMULA FROM FIELD (continued)

2   Click **Edit** menu .... `Alt` + `E`

3.   Click **Clear Formula** .... `E`

Change Field Name in Form View

1.   Select field to change.

2.   Type new field name ....*field name:*
followed by a colon (:).

> *NOTE:*   *Field names may be up to 15 characters long but may not begin with single quotation marks (').*

3.   Press .... `⏎`

Change Field Name in List View

1.   Select field to change.

2   Click **Edit** menu .... `Alt` + `E`

3.   Click **Field Name** .... `N`

4.   Type new name...*name*

> *NOTE:*   *Field names may be up to 15 characters long but may not begin with single quotation marks (').*

5.   Click **OK**.. `⏎`

FORMAT FIELDS

Change Field Size in Form View

Mouse

1.   Select field to change.

2   Click and drag on small square at bottom right corner.

(continued...)

CHANGE FIELD SIZE IN FORM VIEW (continued)

Keystrokes

1. Select field to change.

2. Click **Format** menu .... `Alt` + `T`

3. Click **Field Size** .... `Z`

4. Type number of characters . ...*number*
   for field width.

   NOTE: A field may be up to 325 characters wide.

5. Click **Height** .... `Alt` + `E`

6. Type number of lines ....*number*
   in height.

   NOTE: A field may be up to 325 lines long.

7. Click **OK**.. `↵`

Change Field Width in List View

Mouse

Click and drag border to right of field name.

Keystrokes

1. Select field to change.

2. Click **Format** menu .... `Alt` + `T`

3. Click **Field Width**.. `W`

   OR

   Click **Record Height**.. `H`

(continued...)

CHANGE FIELD WIDTH IN LIST VIEW (continued)

4. Type number of characters ....*number*
    for field size or number of lines for row height.

    NOTE: *A field in list view may be up to 79 characters wide
    and a record can be from 4 to 405 high.*

5. Click **OK**.. ⏎

Change List View Field Size to Fit Largest Entry

Double-click field name whose width you would like to change.

OR

Double-click field number whose height you would like to change.

OR

a. Click **Format** menu .... **Alt** + **T**

b. Click **Field Width**.. **W**

    OR

    Click **Field Height** .... **H**

c. Click **Best Fit**... **Alt** + **B**
    to select (⊠).

d. Click **OK**.. ⏎

Hide Field in List View

    NOTE: *A field hidden in List view will remain visible in
    Form view.*

Mouse

Click and drag right field border to left field border.

(continued...)

CHANGE LIST VIEW FIELD SIZE TO FIT LARGEST ENTRY (continued)

Keystrokes

1. Select field to hide.

2. Click **Format** menu .... `Alt` + `T`

3. Click **Field Width** .... `W`

4. Type zero .... `0`
   in text box.

5. Click **OK** .... `←┘`

Display Field

1. Press .... `F5`

2. Click **Names** .... `Alt` + `N`

3. Select name of field .... `↓`
   to display.

4. Click **OK** .... `←┘`

5. Click **Format** menu .... `Alt` + `T`

6. Click **Field Width** .... `W`

7. Type new field width .... *number*
   in text box.

8. Click **OK** .... `←┘`

Hide Field Name in Form View

1. Select field name to hide.

2. Click **Format** menu .... `Alt` + `T`

(continued...)

HIDE FIELD NAME IN FORM VIEW (continued)

3. Click **Show Field Name** to clear .... `H`

Display Field Name

1. Select nameless field.

2. Click **Format** menu .... `Alt` + `T`

3. Click **Show Field Name** .... `N`
    to select (✓).

FORMAT FORM

Add Rectangle

1. Place insertion point at top left corner of desired rectangle.

2. Click **Insert** menu.............................. `Alt` + `I`

3. Click **Rectangle**.. `N`

    To change size of rectangle:

    a. Click rectangle to select.

    b. Drag corner or center edge square to new size.

Add Border

1. Select element(s) to frame.

2. Click **Format** menu .... `Alt` + `T`

3. Click **Border**... `B`

4. Click **Line Style** .... `I`

(continued...)

ADD BORDER (continued)

5. Select desired style .... `↓`

   NOTE: Choose empty style to remove a border.

6. Click **C**olor... `C`

7. Choose desired color .... `↓`

8. Click **OK**... `↵`

Add Color and Pattern

1. Select element to color.

   OR

   To color entire form:

   Do not select an element.

2. Click **Forma**t menu .... `Alt` + `T`

3. Click **P**attern... `P`

4. Choose desired pattern .... `↓`

   To remove color or pattern:

   Choose None.

5. Click **F**oreground list box .... `Alt` + `F`

6. Choose desired foreground color .... `↓`

7. Click **B**ackground list box......................... `Alt` + `B`

8. Choose desired background color .... `↓`

9. Click **OK** twice... `↵`

EDIT FIELD ENTRY

1. Select field entry to edit.

2. Click formula bar.

   OR

   Press F2

   To Move Insertion Point to Beginning of Text:

   Click left of first letter.

   OR

   Press .... Home

   To Move Insertion Point to End of Text:

   Click right of last letter.

   OR

   Press .... End

   To Move Insertion Point to Left or Right:

   Click at desired position.

   OR

   Press.. ←, →

   To Select Characters:

   Click and drag over desired characters.

   OR

   Press .... Shift + ←, →

To Delete Selected Characters

a. Select characters to delete.

b. Press.. Del

3. Press Enter .... Enter

OR

Click .... ☑

Replace Field Entry in Form or List View

1   Select field entry to replace.

2. Type new entry .... *field entry*

3. Press Enter .... Enter

OR

Click .... ☑

USE NUMBERS AND DATES

Enter Number or Date Series in List

In List view, this feature will automatically enter numbers or dates that progress in even increments into adjacent records.

1. Enter starting number or date in first field.

2. Press .... ⏎

3. Select fields to receive new data.

4. Click **E**dit menu .... Alt + E

5. Click **F**ill Series I

(continued...)

ENTER NUMBER OR DATE SERIES IN LIS (continued)

6. Choose desired unit of measurement to select (⊚):

   - <u>N</u>umber .... `N`

   - <u>D</u>ay .... `D`

   - <u>W</u>eekday .... `W`

   - <u>M</u>onth .... `M`

   - <u>Y</u>ear .... `Y`

7. Click <u>S</u>tep by .... `S`

8. Type increment size .... *number*

9. Click **OK** .... `↵`

Use Mathematical Functions in Formula

A function is a mathematical equation that can also be used to manipulate text. (See the Appendix, page 261, for a list of functions.)

1. Select field to contain formula.

2. Type .... `=`

3. Type desired function .... *function*

4. Type .... `(`

5. Type fields to calculate, separated by commas.

6. Type .... `)`

7. Press .... `↵`

   OR

   Click .... `✓`

174

Date and Time Formats

Dates and times may be used in formulas, but they must be typed in Works formats.

LONG   **EXAMPLES**

Month, day, year..July 23, 1993

Month, year..July 1993

Month, day..July 23

Month ....July

SHORT

Month, day, year 7/23/93

Month, year 7/93

Month, day 7/23

24-HOUR

Hour, minute, second...16:30:00

Hour, minute 16:30

12-HOUR

Hour, minute, second ....4:30:00 AM

Hour, minute..4:30 AM

Enter Date or Time

1. Place insertion point in blank field.

2. Type date or time using Works format.

(continued...)

ENTER DATE OR TIME (continued)

3. Press .... ⏎

    OR

    Click .... ☑

Date or time will be displayed in previously selected format.

Change Date or Time Format

1. Select cell or range to change.

2. Click **Format** menu .... Alt + T

3. Click **Number** .... N

4. Click **Date** .... D

    OR

    Click **Time** .... T

5. Select desired format .... ↓

6. Click **OK** .... ⏎

Insert Current Date or Time

Inserts the date or time, which will not change if you recalculate the spreadsheet.

1. Select cell where date or time is to appear.

2. Press.. Ctrl + ;
    to enter current date.

    OR

    Press.............................. Ctrl + Shift + ;
    to enter current time.

(continued...)

INSERT CURRENT DATE OR TIME (continued)

3. Press .... ⏎

    OR

    Click .... ☑

4. Format as desired.

EDIT RECORDS

Add Record in Form View

1. Select record at location of desired new record position.

2. Click **I**nsert menu.. `Alt` + `I`

3. Click **R**ecord .... `R`

Delete Record in Form View

1. View record to delete.

2. Click **I**nsert menu.. `Alt` + `I`

3. Click **D**elete Record .... `D`

Add Record in List View

1. Select record appearing at desired new record position.

2. Click **I**nsert menu.. `Alt` + `I`

3. Click **R**ecord/Field .... `R`

Delete Record in List View

1. Select record to delete.

(continued...)

DELETE RECORD IN LIST VIEW (CONTINUED)

2. Click **I**nsert menu.. `Alt` + `I`

3. Click **D**elete Record/Field .... `D`

Copy Record

– IN FORM VIEW –

1. View record to copy.

    OR

– IN LIST VIEW –

Select record to copy.

2. Click **E**dit menu.. `Alt` + `E`

– IN FORM VIEW –

3. Click **Copy** record.. `Y`

    OR

– IN LIST VIEW –

Click **C**opy.. `C`

4. Select blank or other record to receive copied record.

    NOTE: The pasted letter will replace any information in the selected record.

    OR

    Place insertion point in another document to receive copied record

(continued...)

COPY RECORD (continued)

5. Click .... 📋

    OR

    a. Click **E**dit menu .... `Alt` + `E`

    b. Click **P**aste .... `P`

    OR

    Click **P**aste Record .... `P`

    OR

    Press .... `Shift` + `Ins`

Move Record in List View

– IN FORM VIEW –

1. View record to copy.

    OR

– IN LIST VIEW –

    Select record to copy.

2. Click **E**dit menu .... `Alt` + `E`

– IN FORM VIEW –

3. Click **Cut Record** .... `D`

    OR

– IN LIST VIEW –

    Click **Cut** .... `T`

(continued...)

MOVE RECORD IN LIST VIEW (continued)

4. Select blank or other record to receive copy.

   NOTE: *Works will replace selected record with copied*
   record.

5. Click.. 📋

   OR

   a. Click **E**dit menu... Alt + E

   b. Click **P**aste... P

   OR

   Press... Shift + Ins

Hide Record

– IN FORM VIEW –

1. View record to hide

   OR

– IN LIST VIEW –

   Select record or records to hide.

2. Click **V**iew menu.................................... Alt + V

3. Click Hi**d**e Record .... D

Switch Hidden and Displayed Records

1. Click **V**iew menu.................................... Alt + V

2. Click S**w**itch Hidden Records................................. W

Display All Records

1. Click **View** menu .... `Alt` + `V`

2. Click **Show All Records** .... `A`

FORMAT TEXT

Select Font

Toolbar

1. Select fields, labels or field names to change.

2. Click drop-down list button .... `↓`
   to right of current font name.

3. Choose desired font .... `↓`

4. Click drop-down list button .... `↓`
   to right of current font size.

5. Select size .... `↓`

Shortcut Keys

1. Press .... `Ctrl` + `F`

2. Choose desired font .... `↓`

3. Press .... `↵`

Change Font and Size Simultaneously

1. Select text to change.

2. Click **Format** menu .... `Alt` + `T`

3. Click **Font & Style** .... `F`

(continued...)

CHANGE FONTAND SIZE SIMULTANEOUSLY (continued)

4. Select desired font.................................. ⬆ , ⬇

5. Choose desired Styles from the following:

   • Bold... Alt + B

   • Italic .... Alt + I

   • Underline....................................... Alt + U

   • Strikethrough .... Alt + T

6. Choose desired size .... Alt + S , ⬇

7. Choose desired color...................... Alt + O , ⬇

8. Click **OK**... ↵

Underline

1. Select fields to underline.

2. Click... U

   OR

   Press.. Ctrl + U

Bold

1. Select fields to bold.

2. Click... B

   OR

   Press.. Ctrl + B

Italics

1. Select fields to italicize.

2. Click.. $\boxed{\textit{I}}$

   OR

   Press... $\boxed{\text{Ctrl}}$ + $\boxed{\text{I}}$

Return to Plain Text

1. Select fields to make plain text.

2. Press................................. $\boxed{\text{Ctrl}}$ + $\boxed{\text{Space}}$

Align Text Horizontally

Unless otherwise specified, text in database fields will be left-aligned and numbers will be right-aligned. Text and numbers may be left-aligned, right-aligned or centered by using Indents & Spacing dialog box, the Toolbar or shortcut keystrokes.

1. Select fields, field names or labels to align.

2. Click **Format** menu .... $\boxed{\text{Alt}}$ + $\boxed{\text{T}}$

3. Click **A**lignment.. $\boxed{\text{A}}$

4. Choose desired alignment:

   • **L**eft... $\boxed{\text{L}}$

   • **R**ight.. $\boxed{\text{R}}$

   • **C**enter .... $\boxed{\text{C}}$

   • **G**eneral .... $\boxed{\text{G}}$

5. Click **S**lide to Left .... $\boxed{\text{S}}$
   to close up empty space in previous field, if desired.

6. Click **OK**.. $\boxed{\leftarrow}$

Align List View Text Vertically

1. Select fields, field names or labels to align.

2. Click **Format** menu .... `Alt` + `T`

3. Click **Alignment** .... `A`

4. Choose desired alignment:

    *   **Top** .... `T`

    *   **Center** .... `E`

    *   **Bottom** .... `B`

5. Click **OK** .... `←`

Wrap Text in List View

1. Select fields, field names or labels to align.

2. Click **Format** menu .... `Alt` + `T`

3. Click **Alignment** .... `A`

4. Click **Wrap Text** .... `W`
    to select (⊠).

5. Click **OK** .... `←`

EDIT TEXT

Drag and Drop to Move Field Entry

Field entries may be moved, by the drag and drop method, from one place to another in a document or from one file to another. When moved to another Works database, the entries and formatting are copied. When moved to another application, the information may be embedded (see page 67).

184

DRAG AND DROP TO MOVE FIELD ENTRY (continued)

If moving information from one file to another:

1. Arrange screen to view both windows.

2. Select text or object to move.

3. Hold mouse button and drag to new location with insertion point on selection. Insertion point will change appearance to indicate selection is being dragged.

   NOTE: *If insertion point changes to a circle with a slash, it indicates the selection cannot be moved to that location with this method.*

4. Release mouse button.

Copy Field Entry to Clipboard

1   Select text to copy.

2. Click.. 🖺

   OR

   a. Click **E**dit menu................................. `Alt` + `E`

   b. Click **C**opy.. `C`

   OR

   Press.. `Ctrl` + `C`

CUT FIELD ENTRY TO CLIPBOARD

1. Select text to cut.

2. Click .... ✂

   OR

   a. Click **E**dit menu... `Alt` + `E`

(continued...)

CUT FIELD ENTRY TO CLIPBOARD (continued)

b. Click **Cut**.. `T`

OR

Press... `Ctrl` + `X`

Paste Field Entry from Clipboard

1. Place insertion point where text is to be pasted.

2. Click.. 📋

   OR

   a. Click **Edit** menu....................................... `Alt` + `E`

   b. Click **Paste**... `P`

   OR

   Press... `Ctrl` + `V`

Copy Field Entry to Adjacent Fields in List View

1. Select field entries to copy and fields to fill.

   *NOTE: Works will replace field entries with copied field
            entry.*

2. Click **Edit** menu....................................... `Alt` + `E`

3. Click **Fill Down**.. `W`

   OR

   Click **Fill Right**.. `H`

186

Change Number Format in Form, List or Report View

1. Select cells to format.

2. Click **Format** menu .... `Alt` + `T`

3. Click **Number** .... `N`

4. Click desired format from the following option:

   - **General** .... `G`

   - **Fixed** .... `X`

   - **Currency** .... `U`

   - **Comma** .... `C`

   - **Percent** .... `P`

   - **Exponential** .... `E`

   - **Leading Zeros** .... `L`

   - **Fraction** .... `A`

   - **True/False** .... `R`

   - **Date** .... `D`

   - **Time** .... `I`

   - **Text** .... `T`

5. Type desired number of decimals .... *number*

6. Click **OK** .... `↵`

Use Formula to Automate Field Entry

A formula may be used to enter automatically text or numbers in field of new record. The entry may then be accepted or edited.

(continued...)

USE FORMULA TO AUTOMATE FIELD ENTRY (continued)

1. Select field to contain formula.

2. Type equals sign (=).. `=`

3. Type number ....*number*
   to enter automatically.

   OR

   Type text, enclosed in double quotation marks...............*text*
   to enter automatically.

4. Press .... `↵`

FORMAT RECORDS

Create Field Label in Form View

1. Place insertion point in blank location
   where label is to appear.

2. Type label text ....*text*

   CAUTION: Do not end text with a colon.

3. Press .... `↵`

Move Label in Form View

Click and drag label to new position.

OR

1. Select label to move.

2. Click **Edit** menu............................... `Alt` + `E`

3. Click **Position Selection** .... `I`

(continued...)

MOVE LABEL IN FORM VIEW (continued)

4. Press .... $\boxed{\uparrow}$, $\boxed{\downarrow}$, $\boxed{\leftarrow}$, $\boxed{\rightarrow}$

5. Press .... $\boxed{\leftarrow\!\!\lrcorner}$

Delete Label

1. Select label to delete.

2. Click **I**nsert menu .... $\boxed{Alt}$ + $\boxed{I}$

3. Click **Delete Selection** .... $\boxed{S}$

4. Click **OK** .... $\boxed{\leftarrow\!\!\lrcorner}$
   to confirm.

Move Field in Form View

Click and drag field to new position.

OR

1. Select field to move.

2. Select **E**dit menu .... $\boxed{Alt}$ + $\boxed{E}$

3. Click **Position Selection** .... $\boxed{I}$

4. Press .... $\boxed{\uparrow}$, $\boxed{\downarrow}$, $\boxed{\leftarrow}$, $\boxed{\rightarrow}$

5. Press .... $\boxed{\leftarrow\!\!\lrcorner}$

Turn Snap to Grid on or off

1 Click **Format** menu .... $\boxed{Alt}$ + $\boxed{T}$

2. Click **O**ptions .... $\boxed{O}$

3. Click **Snap to Grid** .... $\boxed{S}$
   to select (✓) or clear.

Move Field in List View

1. Select field to move.

2. Press .... ✂️

   OR

   a. Click **E**dit menu .... Alt + E

   b. Click **Cu**t .... T

3. Select field to appear at right of new field position,
   or select a blank column.

   Columns will move to right to make room for pasted field.

4. **Press** .... 📋

   OR

   a. Click **E**dit menu .... Alt + E

   b. Click **P**aste .... P

SORT DATABASE RECORDS

*Records in a database may be sorted in alphabetical, numerical,
ascending or descending order. Blank entries will follow all other
entries.*

1. Click **T**ools .... Alt + O

2. Click **So**rt **Records** .... R

3. Type field name .... *Field name*
   for first priority sort.

   OR

   Select name .... ⬇️
   from drop-down list.

(continued...)

190

SORT DATABASE RECORDS (continued)

4. Choose desired order to select (⦿):

   • Ascend **A**.. `Alt` + `A`

   • Descend **B**.. `Alt` + `B`

5. Click **2nd Field**, if desired............................ `Alt` + `2`

6. Type or select field name.....................................*Field name*
   for second sort priority

7. Choose desired order to select (⦿):

   • Ascend **C**.. `Alt` + `C`

   • Descend **D**.. `Alt` + `D`

8. Click **3rd Field**, if desired.............................. `Alt` + `3`

9. Type or select field name ....*Field name*
   for third sort priority

10. Choose desired order:

    • Ascend **E**.. `Alt` + `E`

    • Descend **F**.. `Alt` + `F`

11. Click **OK**.. `↵`

Repeat Sort

1. Click **Tools**.. `Alt` + `O`

2. Click **Sort Records**.. `R`

3. Click **OK**.. `↵`

SEARCH FOR RECORDS

Finds specific records in the database containing search values. The ? (question mark) may be used as a wildcard to stand for any one character, and the *(asterisk) may be used to stand for any number of characters. Use the Query method (p. 168) for more complex sorts. Found records may be printed, used to create a report or copied.

1. Click Edit menu... `Alt` + `E`

2. Click Find.. `F`

3. Type text to find .... *text*

4. Choose desired search range option to select (◉):

   • Next record .... `Alt` + `R`
     to display next matching record.

   • All records... `Alt` + `A`
     to display all matching records.

5. Click OK.. `↵`

Repeat Search

Press.. `F7`

Display Records Not Matching Search Text

1. Click View menu..................................... `Alt` + `V`

2. Click Switch Hidden Records.............................. `W`

Display All Records

1. Click View menu..................................... `Alt` + `V`

2. Click Show All Records .... `A`

SEARCH AND REPLACE
MATCHING TEXT OR VALUES

1. Select cells to search.

    To search entire spreadsheet:

    Do not select any cells.

2. Click **Edit** menu...................................... `Alt` + `E`

3. Click **Replace** .... `L`

    – IN THE FIND WHAT TEXT BOX –

4. Type text or number to find ....*text or number*

    – IN THE REPLACE WITH TEXT BOX –

5. Type replacement characters................................*characters*

6. Choose desired **Look By** order to select (◉):

    - Records.. `Alt` + `O`
      to search from each record, one at a time.

    - Fields... `Alt` + `I`
      to search first field in all records,
      then second, etc.

7. Click **Find Next** .... `Alt` + `F`

    If matching characters are found:

    Choose desired option:

    - Replace .... `Alt` + `R`
      to replace and find next occurrences.

    - Find Next.................................... `Alt` + `F`
      to continue without replacing.

(continued...)

SEARCH AND REPLACE MATCHING TEXT OR VALUES (continued)

- Replace <u>A</u>ll .... **Alt** + **A**
  to replace all occurences automatically.

8. Click **Cancel**... **Esc**
   When finished

QUERY DATABASE FOR RELATED RECORDS

*Use a **query** to search for records meeting more specific conditions than possible using **Find**. Also, to find records that meet more than one condition, to find a range of records or to find records that do not match certain values.*

Query Based on up to Three Criteria

1. Click **T<u>o</u>ols** menu.. **Alt** + **O**

2. Click **<u>C</u>reate New Query**.. **C**

   – IN CHOOSE A FIELD TO COMPARE LIST BOX –

3. Choose a field.. **↓** , **↵**

4. Click **How to Compare the Field** list box .... **Alt** + **B**

5. Choose desired method .... **↓** , **↵**
   of comparison.

6. Click **Value to Compare the Field** to text box. **Alt** + **E**

7. Type value ....*value*
   to compare.

8. Choose desired option to compare first query
   sentence with second query sentence, if desired:

(continued...)

QUERY BASED ON UP TO THREE CRITERIA
(continued)

- Click **And** .... `Alt` + `D`
  to find only records matching
  both query sentences.

  OR

- Click **Or**.. `Alt` + `O`
  to find records matching
  either query sentence.

9. Repeat steps 3-7 for second and third query
   senctence, if desired.

10. Click **Apply Now**...................................... `Alt` + `P`

Query Based on More than Three Criteria

Use Query view to design queries based on more than three criteria or
to design queries including mathematical formulas or functions.

– ON TOOLBAR –

1. Click .... 🗇

   OR

   a. Click **Tools** menu .... `Alt` + `O`

   b. Click **Create New Query**............................ `C`

   c. Click **Clear** .... `C`

   d. Click **Query View**..................................... `V`

2. Type query instructions in any fields desired.

   NOTE: See below for query instructions.

(continued...)

QUERY BASED ON MORE THAN THREE CRITERIA (continued)

To see results in form view:

Click .... 🖻

To see results in list view:

Click .... 📊

To see results in print preview:

Click .... 🔍

Search for Records Matching Field Text or Values

Finds records with exactly matching fields when you type text or values. Text to match must be enclosed with double quotation marks. The wildcards question mark (?) for one character, and asterisk (•) for any number of characters may be used in search text. For example, "s?ck" would find field entries sock and sick, "s•ck" would find sock, sick, slack and slick.

Search Using Comparison and Logical Operators in Query View

Comparison and logical operators may be used in combination with each other in Query view. Text, such as names or letters, and dates used with comparison operators must be enclosed in quotation marks, for example: >"7/23/56". Dates are otherwise treated as numbers in query instructions, and may be added and subtracted, etc. Mathematical operators (see page 261) and Works functions (see page 101) may also be used in a query.

Equal to .... =

Not equal to .... < >

Less than .... <

Less than or equal to .... < =

(continued...)

SEARCH USING COMPARISON AND LOGICAL OPERATORS IN QUERY VIEW (continued)

Greater than	`>`
Greater than or equal to	`>` `=`
And	`&`
Or	`|`
Not	`~`

Name Query

1. Click **T**o**o**ls menu... `Alt` + `O`

2. Click **Na**m**e** Query... `M`

3. Select query .... `↑` , `↓`
   to rename.

4. Click **N**ame text box... `Alt` + `N`

5. Type new name ....*new name*

6. Click **R**ename button... `Alt` + `R`

7. Repeat steps 3 to 6 for each query to rename.

8. Click **OK**.. `↵`

Delete Query

1. Click **T**o**o**ls menu... `Alt` + `O`

2. Click **Dele**t**e** Query.. `T`

3. Select query .... `↑` , `↓`
   to delete.

4. Click **D**elete... `Alt` + `D`

5. Click **OK**.. `↵`

Duplicate Query

1   Click **Tools** menu .... `Alt` + `O`

2. Click **Duplicate Query** .... `P`

3. Select query .... `↑` , `↓`
    to duplicate.

4. Click **Name** text box .... `Alt` + `N`

5. Type query name .... *query name*

6. Click **Duplicate** .... `Alt` + `U`

7. Click **OK** .... `⏎`

View Records That Query Did Not Find

1. Click **View** menu .... `Alt` + `V`

2. Click **Switch Hidden Records** .... `W`

Show All Records

1. Click **View** menu .... `Alt` + `V`

2. Click **Show All Records** .... `L`

Repeat Last Query

1. Press **F3** .... `F3`

    OR

    a. Click **View** menu .... `Alt` + `V`

(continued...)

REPEAT LAST QUERY (continued)

    b. Click **Apply Query**.. `P`

2. Select query... `↓`
    to apply.

3. Click **OK**.. `↵`

Hide One Record

1. View or highlight record to hide.

2. Click **View** menu............................... `Alt` + `V`

3. Click **Hide Record** .... `D`

Edit Query

1. Click **View** menu............................... `Alt` + `V`

2. Click **Query** .... `Q`

3. Change query instructions, as desired.

4. Press .... `↵`

To see results in Form view:

Click .... 🗗

To see results in list view:

Click.. ▤

To see results in print preview:

Click .... 🔍

UNLOCK OR LOCK FIELD IN FORM OR LIST VIEW

Locks protect field contents from accidental changes. The Works default setting locks all fields, but protection is not turned on and the locks are not in effect.

1. Select cells to lock.

2. Click **Format** menu .... `Alt` + `T`

3. Click **Protection** .... `R`

4. Click **Locked** .... `L`
   to select (☒) or clear (☐).

5. Click **OK** .... `↵`

Turn Protection On or Off

1. Click **Format** menu .... `Alt` + `T`

2. Click **Protection** .... `R`

3. Click **Protect Data** .... `P`
   to select (☒) to protect locked entries
   or clear (☐) to turn off protection.

4. Click **OK** .... `↵`

PROTECT FORM DESIGN

This feature locks the form design only. Text and values may still be entered in fields.

1. View database in Form view .... 🗇

2. Click **Format** menu .... `Alt` + `T`

(continued...)

PROTECT FORM DESIGN (continued)

3.   Click **Protection**... `R`

4.   Click **Protect Form** .... `R`
     to select (⊠).

CREATE REPORT

> *NOTE:*   *A database may be printed from List or Form view,*
> *or a specific report form may be created and saved.*
> *The report form is more flexible and variable than*
> *printing from Form or List view, with complex*
> *sorting, grouping, calculation or other features.*

1.   View database for which you want to create report.

2.   Click **Tools** menu... `Alt` + `O`

3.   Click **Create New Report** .... `N`

– IN REPORT TITLE TEXT BOX –

4.   Type title for report ....*title*

5.   Click **Field** list box.. `Tab`

6.   Select first field .... `↓`
     to include.

7.   Click **Add**... `Alt` + `A`

8.   Repeat steps 5 to 7 for each field to include.

     To add all fields:

     Click **Add All** .... `Alt` + `D`

     To remove field:

(continued...)

CREATE REPORT (continued)

a. Click **Fields in Report** list box .... `Alt` + `F`

b. Select field .... `↓`
   to remove.

c. Click **Remove** .... `Alt` + `R`

9.   Click **OK** .... `↵`

10. Click **Fields in Report** .... `Alt` + `F`
     to select field to calculate, if desired.

11. Select field .... `↓`
     to calculate.

If calculating a field:

a. Click statistics desired to select (⊠):

  • **S**um .... `Alt` + `S`

  • **A**verage .... `Alt` + `A`

  • **C**ount .... `Alt` + `C`

  • **M**inimum .... `Alt` + `M`

  • Ma**x**imum .... `Alt` + `X`

  • **St**andard Deviation .... `Alt` + `T`

  • **V**ariance .... `Alt` + `V`

b. Click desired position for result to select (⊠):

  • **U**nder Each Column .... `Alt` + `U`

  • T**o**gether in Rows .... `Alt` + `O`

(continued...)

CREATE REPORT (continued)

12. Repeat steps 10-11 for each field to calculate.

13. Click **OK** twice..

Switch Database View

1. Click **View** menu.. `Alt` + `V`

2. Click **Form**.. `F`

   OR

   Click **List**... `L`

   OR

   Click **Report**.. `R`

PARTS OF REPORT

Gives you greater control of the printed database. Report parts are labeled at the left of the report window. The parts include anything in the related row(s).

PART	FUNCTION
Title	Prints only at top of first page.
Headings	Print at top of every page.
Record	Includes fields to print and repeats on each page, as space permits.
Intr *fieldname*	The starting point for a grouping of sorted records, it is blank or includes a heading. (Optional)

(continued...)

PARTS OF REPORT (continued)

Summ *fieldname* The ending of a group of sorted records, it includes a statistical summary. (Optional)

Summary Appears at the end of a report and includes statistical summaries.

FORMAT PAGES

Change Column Width or Row Height in Report View

Mouse

Click and drag border to right of column letter or below row number to desired new size.

Keystrokes

1. Select field to change.

2. Click **Format** menu .... `Alt` + `T`

3. Click **Column Width** .... `W`

   OR

   Click **Row Height** .... `H`

4. Type number of characters ....*number* for column width or lines for row height.

   NOTE: *A column in report view may be up to 79 characters wide; a row may be 4 to 409 characters high.*

5. Click **OK** .... `←`

FORMAT REPORT

Add Blank Row to Report

1. Select row(s) where new row(s) is to be inserted.

2. Click **I**nsert menu...................................... `Alt` + `I`

3. Click **R**ow/Column .... `R`

4. Select row type .... `↓`
   to include.

5. Click **OK**.. `↵`

Add Blank Column to Report

1. Select column(s) where new column(s) are to be inserted.

2. Click **I**nsert menu...................................... `Alt` + `I`

3. Click **R**ow/Column .... `R`

Delete Row or Column from Report

> *NOTE:* *Deleting a row or column removes any text or fields contained in it from the report, but not from the database itself.*

1. Select rows or columns to delete.

2. Click **I**nsert menu...................................... `Alt` + `I`

3. Click **D**elete Row/Column................................... `D`

Add Text to Report

1. Place insertion point where text is to appear.

2. Type text..*text*

3. Press .... `↵`

Add Field Name Label to Report

1   Place insertion point at desired location.

> *NOTE:*   *Field name labels are usually placed in Heading or*
> *Intr rows to identify data entries that appear below.*

2. Click **I**nsert menu.................................... `Alt` + `I`

3. Click **Field Name** .... `N`

4. Select desired field label.. `↓`

5. Click **OK**.. `↵`

Change Report Entry

1. Select entry to change.

2. Type new entry or instruction..................*entry or instruction*

3. Press .... `↵`

    OR

    Click.. `☑`

Edit Report Entry

1. Select entry to change.

2. Click desired location in formula bar.

    OR

    Press .... `F2`

3. Edit entry as desired (see below).

(continued...)

EDIT REPORT ENTRY (continued)

4. Press .... ⏎

    OR

    Click .... ☑️

Report Editing Keystrokes

To move insertion point to beginning of text:

Click left of first character.

OR

Press .... Home

To move insertion point to end of text:

Click right of last character.

OR

Press .... End

To move insertion point left or right:

Click desired location.

OR

Press... ←, →

To select characters:

Click and drag over desired characters.

OR

Press .... Shift + ←, Shift + →

(continued...)

REPORT EDITING KEYSTROKES (continued)

To delete selected characters:

Press .... Del

Clear Report Entry

1. Select each entry to clear.

   NOTE: Entire columns or rows may be selected.

2. Press .... Del

   OR

   a. Click **E**dit menu .... Alt + E

   b. Click **Cl**ear .... E

Move Report Entry, Column or Row

1. Select entry, column or row to move.

2. Press .... ✂

   OR

   a. Click **E**dit menu .... Alt + E

   b. Click **Cu**t .... T

3. Place insertion point at upper left corner of
   desired new location.

   *NOTE: Moved items will fill downward and to the right
   over existing items.*

(continued...)

MOVE REPORT ENTRY, COLUMN OR ROW (continued)

4. Press .... 📋

   OR

   a. Click **E**dit menu.............................. `Alt` + `E`

   b. Click **P**aste....................................... `P`

Add Field to Report

> *NOTE: Adding a field entry instruction tells Works to include all the entries (data) for that field in the report.*

1. Place insertion point at desired location.

   > *NOTE: Field entry instructions are usually placed in record rows.*

2. Click **I**nsert menu............................... `Alt` + `I`

3. Click **Field Entr**y.................................. `Y`

4. Select field name .... `↓`
   to include.

5. Click **OK**.. `↵`

Add Calculation Formula to Report

> *NOTE: Calculation formulas inserted in Summfieldname rows will be performed on records in each sorted group. Calculation formulas inserted in Summary rows are performed on all records in the report.*

1. Select location in Summ*fieldname*
   row (see page. 176), or a Summary row.

(continued...)

ADD CALCULATION FORMULA TO REPORT
(continued)

2. Click **Insert** menu....................................... `Alt` + `I`

3. Click **Field Summary** .... `S`

4. Select field name .... `↓`
   to use.

5. Click a statistical operation to select (◉):

   • **Sum**.. `Alt` + `S`
     to total all entries.

   • **Avg**.. `Alt` + `A`
     to average all values.

   • **Count**.. `Alt` + `C`
     to count number of entries.

   • **Max**.. `Alt` + `X`
     to find largest value.

   • **Min**.. `Alt` + `M`
     to find smallest value.

   • **Std**.. `Alt` + `D`
     to calculate standard deviation.

   • **Var**.. `Alt` + `V`
     to calculate variance.

6. Click **OK**.. `↵`

Add Arithmetic Calculation to Report

> *NOTE:* *Arithmetic calculations inserted in Summfieldname rows will be performed on records in each sorted group. Arithmetic calculations inserted in Summary rows are performed on all records in the report.*

(continued...)

ADD ARITHMETIC CALCULATION TO REPORT (continued)

1. Select location in Summ*fieldname*
   row (see page. 176) or Summary row.

2. Type an equal sign .... `=`

3. Type formula, using field names,
   mathematical symbols and numbers.

   Subtraction .... `-`

   Addition .... `+`

   Multiplication .... `*`

   Division .... `/`

4. Press .... `↵`

   OR

   Click .... `☑`

FORMAT NUMBERS

1. Select entries to format.

2. Click **Format** menu .... `Alt` + `T`

3. Click **Number** .... `N`

4. Click desired format to select (◉):

   • General .... `G`

   • Fixed .... `X`

   • Currency .... `U`

(continued...)

FORMAT NUMBERS (continued)

- Comma C
- Percent .... P
- Exponential .... E
- Leading Zeros L
- Fraction .... A
- True/False .... F
- Date .... D
- Time I
- Text .... T

5. Type desired number .... *number* of decimals.

6. Click **OK** .... ←

Change Standard Number of Decimal Places

1. Click **Tools** menu .... Alt + O

2. Click **Options** .... O

3. Click **Default Number of Decimals** .... B

4. Type desired default .... *number* for most number formats.

5. Click **OK** .... ←

FORMAT ENTRIES

Change Alignment

Works automatically aligns entries containing text to the left and entries containing numbers or formulas to the right.

Toolbar

1. Select entries to change.

2. Click .... [⊫]
    to left-align entries.

    OR

    Click .... [⊨]
    to right-align entries.

    OR

    Click .... [⊧]
    to center entries.

Wrap Text Inside Field

1. Select entry or entries to change.

2. Click **Forma̱t** menu .... [Alt] + [T]

3. Click **A̱lignment** .... [A]

4. Click **W̱rap Text** .... [W]
    to select (☒).

5. Click **OK** .... [↵]

Center Text or Number over Columns

1. Select columns over which to center text or number.

    *NOTE: Any text or number longer than the column widths
              will be entirely displayed.*

(continued...)

CENTER TEXT OR NUMBER OVER COLUMNS (continued)

2. Click **Forma*t*** menu .... **Alt** + **T**

3. Click **_A_lignment** .... **A**

4. Click **Center _A_cross Selection** .... **A**
   to select.

5. Click **OK**.

Change Vertical Alignment

1. Select entry or entries to change.

2. Click **Forma*t*** menu .... **Alt** + **T**

3. Click **_A_lignment** .... **A**

4. Click desired vertical alignment to select (◉):

   • **_T_op** .... **T**

   • **C_e_nter** .... **E**

   • **_B_ottom** .... **B**

5. Click **OK** .... **↵**

CHANGE FONTS

1. Select entries to change.

2. Click drop-down list button .... **⬇**
   to right of current font name.

3. Choose desired font .... **↓**

4. Press .... **↵**

(continued...)

CHANGE FONTS (continued)

5. Click drop-down list button .... ⬇️
   to right of current font size.

6. Choose desired size .... ⬇️

7. Click **OK** .... ↵

Change Color

1. Select entries to change.

2. Click **Format** menu .... Alt + T

3. Click **Font & Style** .... F

4. Click C**o**lor .... Alt + O

5. Select desired color.. ⬇️

6. Click **OK** .... ↵

Change Font, Size, and Color Simultaneously

1. Select entries to change.

2. Click **Format** menu .... Alt + T

3. Click **Font & Style** .... F

4. Click **Font** .... Alt + F

5. Choose desired font .... ⬇️

6. Click **Size** .... Alt + S

7. Select desired size.. ⬇️

8. Click C**o**lor .... Alt + O

(continued...)

ACHANGE FONT, SIZE, AND COLOR SIMULTANEOUSLY (continued)

9. Select desired color.. ↓

10. Click **OK**.. ↵

Underline

1. Select entries to underline.

2. Click.. U

    OR

    Press.. Ctrl + U

Bold

1. Select entries to bold.

2. Click.. B

    OR

    Press.. Ctrl + B

Italics

1. Select entries to italicize.

2. Click.. I

    OR

    Press.. Ctrl + I

Return to Plain Text

1. Select entries to make plain.

2. Press.. Ctrl + Space

MANAGE REPORTS

Rename Report

1. Click **Tools** menu .... `Alt` + `O`

2. Click **Name Report** .... `A`

3. Select report .... `↓`
    to rename.

4. Click **Name** .... `Tab`

5. Type new name ....*name*

6. Click **Rename** .... `Alt` + `R`

7. Click **OK** .... `↵`

Delete Report

1. Click **Tools** menu .... `Alt` + `O`

2. Click **Delete Report** .... `L`

3. Select report .... `↓`
    to delete.

4. Click **Delete** .... `Alt` + `D`

5. Click **OK** .... `↵`

Duplicate Report

1. Click **Tools** menu .... `Alt` + `O`

2. Click **Duplicate Report** .... `I`

3. Select report .... `↓`
    to duplicate.

(continued...)

DUPLICATE REPORT (continued)

4. Click **N**ame.. `Tab`

5. Type new name...*name*

6. Click **D**uplicate .... `Alt` + `U`

7. Click **O**K.. `↵`

SORT REPORT RECORDS AND SET UP SORT BREAKS

1. Click **T**ools menu....................................... `Alt` + `O`

2. Click So**r**t Records .... `R`

3. Type name ....*field name*
   of first field to sort by.

   OR

   Select field name .... `Alt` + `↓`, `↓`
   from drop down list.

4. Choose desired sort order to select (◉):

   • Ascend **A**.. `Alt` + `A`

   • Descend **B**.. `Alt` + `B`

   To create a grouping:

   Click Break **G**...................................... `Alt` + `G`
   to select (⊠).

   To group entries according to the first letter of the field:

   Click **1**st Letter **I**.............................. `Alt` + `I`
   to select (⊠).   (continued...)

SORT REPORT RECORDS AND SET UP SORT BREAKS (continued)

> **To specify 2nd and 3rd priority sort groups:**
>
> Repeat steps 3-4.

5. Click **OK** .... `←`

PRINT DATABASE

Print Current Record Only in Form View

1. Click **F**ile menu .... `Alt` + `F`

2. Click **P**rint .... `P`

3. Click **C**urrent Record Only .... `Alt` + `U`
   to select (⊙).

Set Printed Appearance of Form View

1. Click **F**ile menu .... `Alt` + `F`

2. Click **Pa**ge Setup .... `G`

3. Click **O**ther Options .... `Alt` + `O`

> **To choose which items to print:**
>
> Click desired choice:
>
> • All **I**tems .... `Alt` + `I`
>
> • Fiel**d** Entries Only .... `Alt` + `D`

5. Click **OK** .... `←`

Slide Field or Label to Left in Form View

Slides a field to the left into the unused space of the preceding field, closing up blank space, for example, to slide a first name and last name together on a mailing label.

(continued...)

219

SLIDE FIELD OR LABEL TO LEFT IN FORM VIEW (continued)

1. Select field or label to slide.

2. Click **Format** menu .... `Alt` + `T`

3. Click **Alignment** .... `A`

4. Click **Slide to Left** .... `Alt` + `S`
   to select (☒).

5. Click **OK** .... `←`

Select Print Options for List View

1. Click **File** menu .... `Alt` + `F`

2. Click **Page Setup** .... `G`

3. Click **Other Options** tab .... `Alt` + `O`

4. Click **Print Gridlines** .... `Alt` + `G`
   to print (☒) or clear (☐).

5. Click **Print record and field label** .... `Alt` + `C`
   to print (☒) or clear (☐).

6. Click **OK** .... `←`

Print One Form on Page (Form View)

1. Click **File** menu .... `Alt` + `F`

2. Click **Page Setup** .... `G`

3. Click **Other Options** tab .... `Alt` + `O`

4. Click **Page breaks between records** .... `Alt` + `B`
   to select (☒).

5. Click **OK** .... `←`

Print More than One Form on Page

1. Click **File** menu.................................... `Alt` + `F`

2. Click **Page Setup** .... `G`

3. Click **Other Options** tab .... `Alt` + `O`

4. Click **Page breaks between records**.............. `Alt` + `B`
   to clear (☐).

5. Click **Space Between Records**.................. `Alt` + `P`

6. Type measurement..*number*

7. Click **OK**.. `↵`

Print Only Selected Records in List View

– IN LIST VIEW –

1. Select first group of adjacent records **not** to print.

2. Click **View** menu.................................... `Alt` + `V`

3. Click **Hide Record** .... `D`

   For other records not adjacent:

   Repeat steps 1 to 3 for each group.

4. Click.. 🖨

   OR

   a. Click **File** menu........................... `Alt` + `F`

   b. Click **Print**.. `P`

5. Click **OK**.. `↵`

PRINT REPORT

1. Select records to print using standard Query methods.

PRINT REPORT (continued)

To view query results in List view:

Click .... ⊞

OR

Press F9

2. Click **V**iew menu .... Alt + V

3. Click **R**eport .... R

4. Choose desired report .... ↓

5. Click **OK** .... ↵

6. Click **F**ile menu .... Alt + F

7. Click **P**rint .... P

8. Select desired print option.

9. Click **OK** .... ↵

COPY REPORT OUTPUT TO ANOTHER LOCATION

1. View report to copy.

2. Select area of report to copy.

3. Click **E**dit menu .... Alt + E

4. Click **Cop**y **Report Output** .... Y

5. View document to receive copy.

6. Place insertion point where report output is to appear.

7. Paste copy .... Ctrl + V

USE CHARTS, DRAWINGS, AND OTHER OBJECTS IN DATABASES

There are several ways to incorporate charts, drawings and other objects in database forms. Objects may be copied (they may be later deleted), linked (they remain joined to the file from which they were copied and are updated when the original is updated) or embedded (the original application may be launched from the word processor).

LINK OBJECTS

Link Spreadsheet Chart

> *NOTE: Linked charts will be updated automatically when the source spreadsheet is updated.*

1. View spreadsheet with chart to link.

2. View database form in second window.

– IN DATABASE WINDOW –

3. Place insertion point at location of linked chart.

4. Click **I**nsert menu.. **Alt** + **I**

5. Click **C**hart .... **C**

6. Click **U**se existing chart .... **Alt** + **U**
    to select (◉).

7. Choose desired **S**preadsheet.............. **Alt** + **S** , **↓**

8. Choose desired **C**hart .... **Alt** + **C** , **↓**

9. Click **OK**.. **↵**

Link Spreadsheet Range to Database File

> *NOTE: Linked spreadsheet ranges will be updated automatically when the source spreadsheet is updated.*

(continued...)

LINK SPREADSHEET CHART (continued)

1. Open spreadsheet with desired range.

   NOTE: Spreadsheet must be named and saved, and range must be named.

2. View database file to which you want to add spreadsheet range.

3. Place insertion point at desired location.

4. Click **Insert** menu.................................... `Alt` + `I`

5. Click **Spreadsheet/table** .... `C`

6. Click **Use existing spreadsheet range** .... `Alt` + `U`
   to select (⦿).

7. Choose desired **Spreadsheet**.............. `Alt` + `S`, `↓`

8. Choose desired **Range** .... `Alt` + `R`, `↓`

9. Click **OK**... `↵`

Change Link to Manual Link

   NOTE: Manual links will be updated only on command.

1. View database file to change.

2. Click **Edit** menu.................................... `Alt` + `E`

3. Click **Links**.. `K`

4. Select linked object.............................. `Alt` + `L`, `↓`
   to change.

5. Click **Manual**...................................... `Alt` + `M`
   to select (⦿).

6. Click **Close** button................................... `Esc`

(continued...)

Update Manual Link

1. Click **E**dit menu...................................... `Alt` + `E`

2. Click **L**inks... `L`

3. Select linked object .... `↓`
   to update.

4. Click **U**pdate **Now**.................................. `Alt` + `U`

5. Click **Close** button.. `⏎`

Link Objects from Other Windows Applications

1. View file with object to link.

2. Select text, cells, drawing or area to link.

3. Press.. `Ctrl` + `C`

4. View database form to receive object.

5. Place insertion point.

6. Click **E**dit menu...................................... `Alt` + `E`

7. Click **Paste S**pecial... `S`

8. Click **Paste L**ink....................................... `Alt` + `L`

9. Click **OK**... `⏎`

EMBED OBJECTS

Embed Spreadsheet

NOTE: *When an object is embedded, it remains attached*
to the application that created it (the application
must be installed on the hard drive). The object
may be edited from the database form.

(continued...)

LINK SPREADSHEET CHART (continued)

1. Place insertion point at desired location in form.

2. Click **Insert** menu.................................... `Alt` + `I`

3. Click **Spreadsheet/Table** .... `P`

4. Click **New Table** .... `Alt` + `N`
   to select (◉).

5. Click **OK**.. `←┘`

6. Type desired information.

   To change size of spreadsheet:

   Click and drag corner to new location.

   To return to database:

   Click document.

   OR

   Press.. `Esc`

Embed Chart

1. Place insertion point at desired location.

2. Click **Insert** menu.................................... `Alt` + `I`

3. Click **Chart**.. `C`

4. Click **New Chart** .... `Alt` + `N`

5. Click **OK**.. `←┘`

6. Click **OK** again .... `←┘`

(continued...)

EMBED CHART (continued)

7. Enter values for chart in spreadsheet.

8. Select range to be charted in spreadsheet.

9. Click **Chart** button at lower left corner of spreadsheet.

10. Choose chart options.

11. Click **OK**...⏎

   To return to database:

   Click database.

   OR

   Press...Esc

Embed Clip Art, Drawing, Note-It or Word Art

1. Place insertion point at desired location.

2. Click **Insert** menu.............................Alt + I

3. Choose desired object type:

   • ClipArt...A

   • WordArt...W

   • Note-It...E

   • Drawing...I

3. Select or create object in tool or application.

4. Quit application or tool by pressing **Escape**
   or using the file menu to quit and return to form window.

Embed Other Object

1. Place insertion point at desired location in form.

2. Click **I**nsert menu.................................. `Alt` + `I`

3. Click **O**bject .... `O`

4. Click **Create New**.................................. `Alt` + `N`

   OR

   a. Click **Create from File** .... `Alt` + `F`

   b. Type **File** name .... `Alt` + `E`, *filename*
      in text box.

5. Click **OK**.. `↵`

EDIT AN OBJECT

Select an Object for Editing

Double-click object.

OR

a. Move insertion point to left of object .... `←`

b. Press.. `Shift` + `→`

Change Object Size

1. Click object to select.

2. Drag handle to desired size.

   *NOTE: Handles are squares appearing at each corner and
   in the center of each edge of a selected object.*

(continued...)

Resize an Object Precisely

1. Click object to select.

2. Click **Format** menu .... `Alt` + `T`

3. Click **Picture/Object** .... `U`

4. Click **Width** text box.............................. `Alt` + `W`

5. Type new width .... *number*

6. Click **Height** text box .... `Alt` + `H`

7. Type new height .... *number*

8. Click Scaling **Width** text box......................... `Alt` + `I`

9. Type new width scale .... *number*

10. Click Scaling **Height** text box......................... `Alt` + `E`

11. Type new height scale .... *number*

12. Click **OK** .... `↵`

Move an Object

1. Click object to select.

   OR

   a. Move insertion point .... `←`
      to left of object.

   b. Press.. `Shift` + `→`

2. Drag object to new position.

   OR

   a. Click **Edit** menu .... `Alt` + `E`

(continued...)

MOVE AN OBJECT (continued)

b. Click **Cut**... `U`

c. Move insertion point to new position.

d. Click **Edit** menu.............................. `Alt` + `E`

e. Click **Paste**.. `P`

SHARE DATABASE FILES WITH OTHER APPLICATIONS

Open Database File from Different Application

> *NOTE:* *Other databases must have been saved as a comma or tab delineated text file in order to be opened by Works.*

1. Click **File** menu.............................. `Alt` + `F`

2. Click **Open Existing File**................................. `O`

3. Click **File Name**............................. `Alt` + `N`

4. Type file to open.

5. Click **OK**.. `←┘`

Open dBase File

1. Click **File** menu.............................. `Alt` + `F`

2. Click **Open Existing File**................................. `O`

3. Click **List Files of Type**............................... `T`

4. Choose **dBase** (*.dbf).

(continued...)

OPEN DATABASE FILE FROM DIFFERENT APPLICATION (continued)

5. Click **File Name**...`Alt` + `N`

6. Type or select file name.

7. Click **OK**..`↵`

SAVE WORKS DATABASE AS TEXT FILE

1. View database to save.

2. Click **File** menu..`Alt` + `F`

3. Click **Save As**...`A`

4. Click **Save File As Type**..............................`Alt` + `T`

5. Choose desired file type:

   - Text & Commas

   - Text & Tabs

   - Text & Tabs (DOS)

6. Click **File Name**...`Alt` + `N`

7. Type filename..*filename*

8. Click **OK**..`↵`

Draw

THE DRAW WINDOW

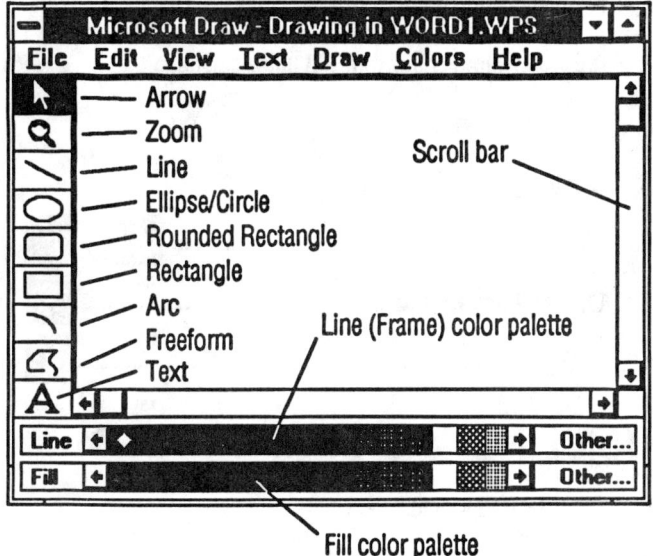

—	Arrow
—	Zoom
—	Line
—	Ellipse/Circle
—	Rounded Rectangle
—	Rectangle
—	Arc
—	Freeform
—	Text

Scroll bar

Line (Frame) color palette

Fill color palette

CREATE DRAWING

> *NOTE:* *Microsoft Draw is available only from within the word processing and database tool, but drawings may be cut or copied and pasted to other Windows applications. Drawings may only be created using a mouse.*

1. Open a new or existing word processing document or database form.

2. Place insertion point where upper left corner of drawing is to appear.

3. Click **Insert** menu.. `Alt` + `I`

(continued...)

CREATE DRAWING (continued)

4. Click **Drawing** .... `I`

5. Choose desired color from **Line color** palette.

6. Choose desired color from **Fill color** palette.

7. Click a drawing tool.

8. Create drawing in Draw window.

9. Click **File** menu .... `Alt` + `F`

10. Click **Exit and Return** .... `X`

11. Click **Yes** .... `Y`

USE LINE AND SHAPE TOOLS

1. Click desired tool to select.

2. Click and drag in Draw window until
    desired line or shape is created.

3. Release mouse button.

    OR

    If using free-form tool, double click.

SELECT LINES, SHAPES OR TEXT

1. Click **Arrow** tool.

2. Click desired item.

(continued...)

SELECT LINES, SHAPES OR TEXT (continued)

To select additional items:

Press .... `Shift`
and click.

FORMAT LINES AND SHAPES

Choose Filled or Unfilled Shapes

1. Click **D**raw menu .... `Alt` + `D`

2. Click **F**illed .... `F`
   to select (✔) or clear.

Choose Framed or Unframed Shapes

1. Click **D**raw menu .... `Alt` + `D`

2. Click **Frame**d.. `D`
   to select (✔) or clear.

Choose Pattern for Fill

1. Click **D**raw menu .... `Alt` + `D`

2. Click **P**attern.. `P`

3. Click desired pattern to select (✔).

Choose Frame Style

1. Click **D**raw menu .... `Alt` + `D`

2. Click **L**ine Style .... `L`

(continued...)

CHOOSE FRAME STYLE (continued)

3. Choose desired style:

- Dotted .... `D`

- Dashed .... `A`

- Dash-dot .... `S`

- Dash-dot-dot .... `T`

- Hairline .... `H`

- 1 Point .... `1`

- 2 Point .... `2`

- 4 Point .... `4`

- 6 Point .... `6`

- 8 Point .... `8`

- 10 Point .... `0`

- Other .... `O`

   *NOTE: If Other is chosen, type desired width, then click
   OK.*

Align Shapes to Grid

1. Click Draw menu .... `Alt` + `D`

2. Click **Snap to Grid** .... `R`
    to select (✔).

USE TEXT TOOL

1 Click **Text** tool.

2. Place insertion point in desired location of Draw window.

3. Type text.

STYLE AND ALIGN TEXT

1. Click **Text** tool.

   OR

   Select text to change with **Text** tool.

2. Click **Text** menu .... `Alt` + `T`

3. Click desired text attributes or alignment to select (✔):

   - Plain .... `P`
   - Bold .... `B`
   - Italic .... `I`
   - Underline .... `U`
   - Left .... `L`
   - Center .... `C`
   - Right .... `R`

4. Type text, if desired.

Select Text Font and Size

1   Click **Text** tool

OR

Select text to change with text tool.

2.   Click **T**ext menu .... `Alt` + `T`

3.   Click **F**ont... `F`

4.   Click desired font to select (✔).

5.   Click **T**ext menu .... `Alt` + `T`

6.   Click **S**ize.. `S`

7.   Choose desired size to select (✔).

8.   Type text, if desired.

EDIT DRAWING

Move Lines, Shapes and Text

1.   Click **Arrow** tool.

2.   Click and drag desired object.

Group Several Objects into One

1. Select objects (lines, shapes, text) to group.

2. Click **D**raw menu .... `Alt` + `D`

3. Click **G**roup .... `G`

Ungroup Objects

1. Select object to ungroup.

2. Click **D**raw menu .... `Alt` + `D`

3. Click **U**ngroup .... `U`

Copy Item

1. Select object to copy.

2. Press .... `Ctrl` + `Ins`

   OR

   a. Click **E**dit menu .... `Alt` + `E`

   b. Click **C**opy .... `C`

3. Press .... `Shift` + `Ins`

   OR

   a. Click **E**dit menu .... `Alt` + `E`

   b. Click **P**aste .... `P`

4. Move object to desired location.

Repeat Paste Command with Same Object

1. Press .... Shift + Ins

   OR

   a. Click **E**dit menu .... Alt + E

   b. Click **P**aste

2. Move object to desired location.

Change Overlap of Lines, Shapes and Text

1. Select item to change.

2. Click **E**dit menu .... Alt + E

3. Click **Bring to Front** .... F

   OR

   Click **Send to Back** .... B

View T-Square Guide

1. Click **D**raw menu .... Alt + D

2. Click **Show Guides** .... W
   to select (✓).

Rotate or Flip Items

1. Select item to change.

2. Click **D**raw menu .... Alt + D

3. Click **Rotate/Flip** .... O

4. Click desired action:

   • Rotate **L**eft L

   • Rotate **R**ight .... R

ROTATE OR FLIP ITEMS(continued)

- Flip Horizontal .... H
- Flip Vertical V

USE COLOR PALETTES

Use Color Not on Color Palette

1. Click **Other** box.

2. Choose desired color on color picker.

    *NOTE: Color values may be lightened or darkened by
               clicking and dragging value slider.*

3. Click **OK** .... ⏎

Add a Color to the Color Palette

1. Click **Colors** menu .... Alt + C

2. Click **Edit Palette** .... E

3. Double-click blank palette square.

4. Choose desired color on color picker.

    *NOTE: Color values may be lightened or darkened by
               clicking and dragging value slider.*

5. Repeat steps 3 to 4 as desired.

6. Click **OK** .... ⏎

Save Color Palette

1. Click **C**olors menu .... `Alt` + `C`

2. Click **S**ave Palette .... `S`

3. Type palette name .... *palette name*

4. Click **OK** .... `←`

Retrieve a Saved Palette

1. Click **C**olors menu .... `Alt` + `C`

2. Click **G**et Palette .... `G`

3. Type palette name .... *palette name*

4. Click **OK** .... `←`

Add Object Colors to Palette

1. Select object with colors to add.

2. Click **C**olors menu .... `Alt` + `C`

3. Click **A**dd Colors from Selection .... `A`

ENLARGE OR REDUCE DRAWING VIEW

1. Click **V**iew menu .... `Alt` + `V`

2. Click desired scale:

   - 25% **S**ize .... `S`

   - **5**0% Size .... `5`

   - **7**5% Size .... `7`

(continued...)

ENLARGE OR REDUCE DRAWING VIEW (continued)

- Full Size .... `F`
- 200% Size .... `2`
- 400% Size .... `4`
- 800% Size .... `8`

USE CLIP ART IN DOCUMENT

1. Open desired document.

2. Place insertion point where clip art is to appear.

3. Click **Insert** menu .... `Alt` + `I`

4. Click **Clip Art** .... `A`

5. Choose desired category.

6. Scroll through art, select desired image.

7. Click **OK** .... `↵`

IMPORT A DRAWING FROM ANOTHER APPLICATION

1. Place insertion point at desired location.

2. Click **Insert** menu .... `Alt` + `I`

(continued...)

IMPORT A DRAWING FROM ANOTHER APPLICATION (continued)

3. Click **D**rawing.. `D`

– IN DRAWING WINDOW –

4. Click **F**ile menu.. `Alt` + `F`

5. Click **I**mport Picture .... `I`

6. Select or type desired filename .... `↓`, *filename*

7. Click **OK**.. `↵`

8. Position and size drawing as desired.

9. Click **F**ile menu.. `Alt` + `F`

10. Click E**x**it and return .... `X`

11. Click **Y**es .... `Alt` + `Y`
    to update document.

Communications

THE COMMUNICATIONS WINDOW

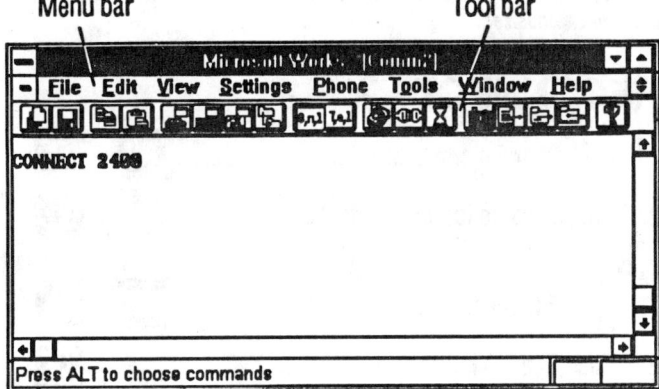

Menu bar   Tool bar

CONNECT 2400

Press ALT to choose commands

BEGIN SESSION

1. Turn on modem.

2. Click **File** menu...................................... Alt + F

3. Click **Create New File** .... N

4. Click **Communications** .... Alt + C

– IN PHONE NUMBER TEXT BOX –

5. Type number ....*number*
   to dial.

   *NOTE: Number should include all prefixes, hyphens are
   optional.*

– IN NAME OF SERVICE TEXT BOX –

6. Type associated name .... Alt + N

(continued...)

244

7. Click **OK** .... ⏎

The modem will dial the number. When the other computer answers, continue as desired.

RECONNECT

1. Click **P**hone menu .... `Alt` + `P`

2. Choose name for number to dial..................... `↓` , ⏎

OR

1. Click **F**ile menu.. `Alt` + `F`

2. Click **O**pen Existing File.................................... `O`

3. Choose or type desired filename.... `Alt` + `N` , *filename*
    in **File N**ame list box.

4. Click **OK**... ⏎

After number is dialed, continue as desired.

REDIAL

1. Click **P**hone menu .... `Alt` + `P`

2. Click **Dial A**gain .... `A`

CANCEL DIALING

– FROM EASY CONNECT OR DIAL STATUS DIALOG BOX –

1. Click **Cancel**... `Esc`

2. Click **OK**... ⏎

ANSWER INCOMING CALLS

1. Click **S**ettings menu .... `Alt` + `S`

2. Click **P**hone .... `Alt` + `P`

3. Click **A**uto Answer .... `Alt` + `A`
   to select (⦿).

4. Click **OK** .... `↵`

QUIT SESSION (HANG UP)

1. Sign off from service, if necessary.

2. Click **P**hone menu .... `Alt` + `P`

3. Click **H**ang Up .... `H`

4. Click **OK** .... `↵`

CONNECT BY CABLE

1. Connect cable to each computer.

2. View communications window.

   NOTE: *Other computer should do the same, or run*
              another application capable of direct connection.

3. Click **S**ettings menu .... `Alt` + `S`

4. Click **C**ommunication .... `Alt` + `C`

5. Select desired **baud rate** and **COM port**.

6. Click **OK** .... `↵`

7. Click **P**hone menu .... `Alt` + `P`

(continued...)

CONNECT BY CABLE (continued)

8. Click **Easy Connect**... `C`

9. Click **OK** .... `↵`

    If running Works on the other computer:

    Repeat steps 3 to 9.

CHANGE SETTINGS

Communication Settings

1. Click **Settings** menu .... `Alt` + `S`

2. Click **Communication** .... `Alt` + `C`

3. Change desired settings *(see below)*.

4. Click **OK** .... `↵`

Port	Connection for modem or cable.
Baud Rate	Data transfer rate; should match other computer's.
Parity	Error checking; should match other computer's.
Ignore Parity	Clear to use parity setting.
Data Bits	Number of bits used for each character; should match other computer's.
Handshake	Controls data flow. Choose **Hardware** option if connecting by cable.
Stop Bits	Number of bits used for end of each character; should match other computer's.

Phone Settings

1. Click **S**ettings menu .... Alt + S

2. Click **P**hone .... Alt + P

3. Change settings as desired *(see below)*.

4. Click **OK** .... ⏎

Phone Number   Number to dial, hyphens optional.

Name of Service   Identifies in phone menu

Connect Option   Redial will retry a busy number, Auto Answer will answer incoming calls.

Redial Attempts   The number of time to retry, if using redial.

Redial Delay   Number of seconds between each redial.

Dial Type   Tone for touch-tone service.

Terminal Settings

1. Click **S**ettings menu .... Alt + S

2. Click **T**erminal .... Alt + T

3. Change settings as desired *(see below)*.

4. Click **OK** .... ⏎

Terminal   Match to other computer's setting.

End of Line   Use to format incoming text.

ISO Translation   Country setting for special characters.

Local Echo   Controls screen display of text.

Wrap Around   Wraps text for window.

SEND TEXT

Send Copied Text

1. Connect to desired computer or service.

2. View document containing text to copy.

3. Select information to copy.

4. Click **Edit** menu... `Alt` + `E`

5. Click **Copy**.. `C`

6. Select communications window.

7. Click **Edit** menu... `Alt` + `E`

8. Click **Paste** Text .... `P`

Send Text File Contents

1. Connect to desired computer or service.

2. Click **Tools** menu.. `Alt` + `O`

3. Click **Send Text** .... `T`

4. Type or select desired filename.

5. Click **OK**.. `↵`

Cancel Transfer

1. Press.. `Esc`

2. Click **OK**.. `↵`

SEND FILE

Set Transfer Protocol

1. Check protocols of other computer.

2. Click **S**ettings menu .... `Alt` + `S`

3. Click T**r**ansfer .... `R`

4. Select matching transfer protocol .... `↓`

5. Click **OK** .... `↵`

Send File

1. Match other computer's transfer protocol *(see above)*.

2. Click T**o**ols menu .... `Alt` + `O`

3. Click **S**end File .... `S`

4. Type or select name of file to send.

5. Click **OK** .... `↵`

Cancel Transfer

1. Press .... `Esc`

2. Click **OK** .... `↵`

SEND BREAK SIGNAL

1. Click **P**hone menu .... `Alt` + `P`

2. Click **B**reak .... `B`

PAUSE COMMUNICATIONS

1. Click **P**hone menu .... `Alt` + `P`

2. Click **P**ause.. `P`

SAVE BUFFER CONTENTS

Text received during a communications session and appears in the communications tool window, and is held in a temporary buffer. It may be reviewed by scrolling, but is not ordinarily saved with the communications document.

If connected to another computer

Click **P**hone menu .... `Alt` + `P`

1. Click **P**ause.. `P`

2. Select text to save.

3. Click **E**dit menu .... `Alt` + `E`

4. Click **C**opy Text .... `C`

5. Open or view document to receive text.

6. Click **E**dit menu .... `Alt` + `E`

7. Click **P**aste .... `P`

CAPTURE TEXT TO FILE

1. Connect to desired computer.

2. Send message to remote computer sending text, if necessary.

3. Click **T**ools menu .... `Alt` + `O`

(continued...)

CAPTURE TEXT TO FILE (continued)

4. Click **Capture Text**.. `C`

5. Type filename ....*filename*
   for captured text.

6. Click **OK**.. `↵`

   To quit saving text:

   Click **Tools** menu............................... `Alt` + `O`

7. Click **End Capture Text**................................ `C`

RECEIVE FILE

1. Match other computer's transfer protocol (see page 213).

2. Send other computer message to begin sending file
   (message will vary).

3. Click **Tools**_menu............................... `Alt` + `O`

4. Click **Receive File** .... `R`

5. Type a filename ....*filename*
   if necessary.

RECORD SCRIPT

Record Sign-on Sequence

1. Click **Tools** menu .... `Alt` + `O`

2. Click **Record Script** .... `D`

3. Click **Sign-On** .... `S`
   to select (⦿).

4. Click **OK** .... `↵`

5. Connect and sign on to other computer or service.

6. Click **Tools** menu .... `Alt` + `O`

7. Click **End Recording** .... `D`

Record Other Procedure

1. Click **Tools** menu .... `Alt` + `O`

2. Click **Record Script** .... `D`

3. Click **Other** .... `O`
   to select (⦿).

4. Type name .... *name*
   for recording.

5. Click **OK** .... `↵`

6. Perform desired sequence.

7. Click **Tools** menu .... `Alt` + `O`

8. Click **End Recording** .... `D`

Play Back Script

1. Connect to computer or service. .... `↓` + `↵`

2. Click T**o**ols_menu .... `Alt` + `O`

3. Select desired script .... `↓` , `↵`
    from list at bottom of menu.

Cancel Recording

1. Click T**o**ols menu .... `Alt` + `O`

2. Click C**a**ncel Recording .... `A`

Cancel Playing

1. Press .... `Esc`

2. Click OK .... `↵`

Rename or Delete Script

> *NOTE:*   *The sign-on script can't be renamed.*

1. Click T**o**ols menu .... `Alt` + `O`

2. Click **E**dit Script .... `E`

3. Select script .... `↓`
    to rename or delete.

4. Click **D**elete .... `Alt` + `D`

    OR

    a. Click **R**ename .... `Alt` + `R`

    b. Type name ....*name*
       in **N**ew **Name** text box.

5. Click OK .... `↵`

Modify Script

1. Click T<u>o</u>ols menu .... `Alt` + `O`

2. Click <u>E</u>dit Script .... `E`

3. Select script .... `↓`
   to change.

4. Click <u>M</u>odify .... `Alt` + `M`

5. Modify script, as desired.

6. Click **OK** .... `↵`

Accessories

USE ELECTRONIC MAIL

USING COMMUNICATIONS TOOL

1. Connect to electronic mail service (page 211).

2. View file containing information to send,
   and select as active window.

3. Click **F**ile menu..**Alt** + **F**

4. Click **S**end ....**S**

5. Check subject line and change, if desired.

6. Type message ....**Alt** + **M** , *message*
   in **M**essage text box, if desired

7. Click **S**end..**Alt** + **S**

ANNOTATE DOCUMENTS

Add Note

1. Place insertion point at desired location
   in word processor or database document.

2. Click **I**nsert menu......................................**Alt** + **I**

3. Click **Not**e**-It** ....**E**

4. Type caption ....*text*
   to appear below note icon.

5. Select desired **P**icture ....**Alt** + **P** , **↓**
   to use as note icon.

(continued...)

ADD NOTE (continued)

6. Click **Type Your Note Here** text box .... `Alt` + `N`

7. Type note text..*text*

8. Click desired note size, to select (◉):

   • Big .... `Alt` + `B`

   • Small .... `Alt` + `S`

9. Click **OK** .... `↵`

Select Note

– USING MOUSE –

Click **Note** icon.

OR

1. Place insertion point to left of note.

– IN WORD PROCESSOR –

2. Press shift .... `Shift` + `→`

   OR

– IN DATABASE FORM –

   Press .... `→`

Read Note

Double-click **Note** icon.

OR

1. Select note.

2. Click **E**dit menu...................................... `Alt` + `E`

3. Click **Microsoft Note-It Object**................................ `O`

4. Click **R**ead .... `⏎`

Close Note

Press .... `Esc`

EDIT NOTE

Note-it objects may be moved, copied, and deleted like other objects (see page 11).

1. Select note.

2. Click **E**dit menu...................................... `Alt` + `E`

3. Click **Microsoft Note-It Object**................................ `O`

4. Click **E**dit .... `E`

5. Make desired changes.

6. Click **OK**.. `⏎`

USE CLIP ART GALLERY

1. Place insertion point at desired location
   in word processor document or database form.

(continued...)

USE CLIP ART GALLERY (continued)

2. Click **I**nsert menu..................................... `Alt` + `I`

3. Click **ClipArt** .... `A`

4. Select desired gallery **C**ategory .... `Alt` + `C`, `↓`
   to view.

5. Scroll through images .... `Shift` + `Tab`
   to view.

6. Select desired image..................... `↑`, `↓`, `←`, `→`

7. Click **OK**.. `↵`

CHANGE IMAGES IN GALLERY

1. View word processor document or database form.

2. Click **I**nsert menu..................................... `Alt` + `I`

3. Click **ClipArt** .... `A`

4. Click **O**ptions .... `Alt` + `O`

5. Click desired selection:

   - **R**efresh... `R`
     to new images and remove old images from gallery.

   - **A**dd .... `A`
     to add new categories.

   - **C**hange a Category... `C`
     to rename or delete categories.

   - **E**dit Picture Info .... `E`
     to edit category and image description.

6. Make changes as desired, following instructions on screen.

Find an Image in Gallery

1. View word processor document or database form.

2. Click **I**nsert menu.. `Alt` + `I`

3. Click **ClipA**rt .... `A`

4. Click **F**ind .... `Alt` + `F`

5. Follow instructions on screen.

6. Click **OK**.. `↵`

CREATE SPECIAL TEXT EFFECTS

Changes text in ways not possible by using font and style features.

Add Word Art

1. Place insertion point in word processor document or database form.

2. Click **I**nsert menu.. `Alt` + `I`

3. Click **W**ordArt .... `W`

4. Type text to use.

5. Make desired changes to text using toolbar buttons *(see below)*.

   OR

   a. Press.. `Esc`

   b. Use menu bar to make changes.

6. Click outside WordArt object...................... `Esc` , `Esc`
   when finished.

EDIT WORD ART

1. Double-click WordArt object.

    OR

    a. Place insertion point to left of WordArt object.

    – IN DATABASE FORM –

    b. Press... →

    OR

    – IN WORD PROCESSOR DOCUMENT –

    Press.. Shift + →

    c. Click **Edit** menu... Alt + E

    d. Click **WordArt Object**..................................... O

    e. Click **Edit**... E

2. Make desired changes to text.

3. Click **Update Display**................................ Alt + U

4. Click outside WordArt object..................... Esc , Esc
    to close dialog box and return to
    document when finished.

Appendix

SPREADSHEET AND DATABASEBUILD FUNCTIONS

DATE AND TIME FUNCTIONS

TO DETERMINE	USE
Date number (may range from January 1, 1900 to June 3, 2079 - represented by Works as a number from 1 to 65534).	DATE(Year,Month,Day)
Day of month Translation of DATE to actual day (an integer from 1 to 31).	DAY(DateNumber)
Month Translation of DATE to actual month.	MONTH(DateNumber)
Year Translation of DATE to actual year.	YEAR(DateNumber)
A time number (may range from 0:00:00 or 12:00:00 p.m. through 23:59:59 or 11:59:59 p.m. - represented by Works as a number from 0.0 through 0.999).	TIME(Hour,Minute,Second)
Hour of the day Translation of time number to actual hour of day.	HOUR(TimeNumber)
Minute of the hour Translation of time number to actual minute of indicated hour.	MINUTE(TimeNumber)
Second of minute Translation of time number to actual second of indicated minute.	SECOND(TimeNumber)
Numbers for current date/time (yields date and time numbers for current date and time).	NOW( )

MATHEMATICAL FUNCTIONS

TO DETERMINE   **USE**

Radian measure of the angle:

- whose Cosine is the indicated number.   ACOS(Number)

- whose Sine is the indicated number.   SIN(Number)

- whose Tangent is the indicated number.   ATAN(Number)

- whose Tangent is defined by x_ & y_   ATAN2(x,y)
  coordinates.

Trigonometry ratio values for angles expressed
in radian measure of:

Cosine	COS(Angle Measure)
Sine	SIN(Angle Measure)
TangentCOS(Angle Measure)	TAN(Angle Measure)

Approximate value of Π.   PI()

Value of e (=2.71828) raised to the   EXP(x)
power of x.

Value of the natural logarithm of   LN(Number)
(base e) of a number.

Value of the common logarithm   LOG(Number)
(base 10) of a number.

Positive value of a number.   ABS(Number).

Integer part of a number.   INT(Number).

Rounded off value of a number to the   ROUND(Number,
left or right of a decimal point.   Round Condition)

(continued...)

MATHEMATICAL FUNCTIONS (continued)

Note:	*If round condition is a:0 (zero).*
	Positive value.
	Negative value.

Note: If round condition is a:0 (zero).   *# is rounded to nearest integer*

Positive value.   *# is rounded to right of decimal*

Negative value.   *# is rounded to the left of decimal*

A random number from 0 to 1, but not including 1.   RAND()

Remainder when 2 numbers are divided (numerator/denominator).   MOD(Numerator, Denominator)

Square root of a positive number.   SQRT(Number)

STATISTICAL FUNCTIONS

TO DETERMINE	USE
Average of numbers in range(s) of cells.	AVG(Range or Ranges)
Number of data entries in ranges(s) of cells.	COUNT(Range or Ranges)
Maximum value in range(s) of cells	MAX(Range or Ranges)
Minimum value in range(s) of cells	MIN(Range or Ranges)
Standard deviation in range(s) of cells	STD(Range or Ranges)
Sum of all values in range(s) of cells	SUM(Range or Ranges)
Variance of values in range(s) of cells	VAR(Range or Ranges)

LOGICAL FUNCTIONS

TO DETERMINE	USE
Error value (Error).	ERR()
Logical value of 0 (false) in a formula.	FALSE()
Logical value of 1 (true) in a formula.	TRUE()
An alternate course of action based on the truth value of a condition.	IF(Condition,Value If True, Value If False)
Logical value of 1 (true) or 0 (false) in a test if cell value contains ERR.	ISERR(Cell Value)
Numeric value N/A (not applicable) will display if true.	NA()
Logical value of 1 or 0 if cell value contains N/A.	ISNA(Cell Value)

FINANCIAL FUNCTIONS

TO DETERMINE	USE
Number of compounding periods needed for the value of an investment to grow to a designated future value.	CTERM(Rate Per Year, Future Value,Present Value)
Future value of an annuity of equal payments earning a fixed rate of interest compounded over a given term.	FV(Payment,Rate,Term)
Present value of an annuity of equal payments earning a fixed rate of interest over a given term.	PV(Payment,Rate,Term)
Amount of each payment based on a fixed rate of interest over a given term.	PMT(Principal,Rate,Term)

FINANCIAL FUNCTIONS (continued)

Description	Function
Rate needed for an investment to grow to a given value over a given term.	RATE(FutureValue, PresentValue,Term)
Number of compounding periods needed for an investment to grow to a given future value for a given rate of interest.	TERM(Payment,Rate, FutureValue)
Internal rate of return for a cash flow series in a given range based on guessed percent of return.	IRR(Guess, RangeReference)
Net present value of a series of cash flow payments.	NPV(Rate, RangeReference)
Double-declining balance method of depreciation calculation for a given period of time.	DDB(Cost,Salvage, Life,Period)
Straight-line depreciation calculation for one period.	SLN(Cost,Salvage,Life)
Sum-of-years-digits method to determine the amount of depreciation for a specific period.	SYD(Cost,Salvage, Life,Period)

LOOKUP AND REFERENCE FUNCTIONS

Description	Function
Matches 0,1,etc. in choice cell to display options listed.	CHOOSE(Choice, Option0,Option 1,)
Number of columns in a given range.	COLS(Range)
Number of rows in a given range.	ROWS(Range)
Value in a cell in a given range at a specific numerically stated column and row within that range.	INDEX(RangeReference, Column,Row)

(continued...)

LOOKUP AND REFERENCE FUNCTIONS (continued)

An entry of a table using:

- The top row of the range to find a value, less than or equal to the look up value, and then down that column to the indicated row.

  HLOOKUP(LookupValue, RangeReference, Column Number)

- The left-most column of the range to find a value less than or equal to the look up value and then goes right to the indicated column.

  VLOOKUP(LookupValue, RangeReference, Column Number)

TEXT FUNCTIONS

NOTE: *When using text as Textvalue, enclose in double quotation marks. It is not necessary to enclose a range reference used as Textvalue.*

TO DETERMINE	USE
• If text values are identical	EXACT(textvalue0, textvalue1)
• Find one text value within another	FIND(Findtext, Searchtext, Offset)
• Leftmost characters from Textvalue	LEFT(Textvalue, length)
• Length of phrase	LENGTH(Textvalue)
• Convert to lowercase	LOWER(Textvalue)
• Extract characters from Textvalue	MID(Textvalue, Offset,Length)
• Give entry in first cell of range a value. Returns 0 if cell contains text.	N(Rangereference)

(continued...)

TEXT FUNCTIONS (continued)

- Capitalize first letter of each word
  and converts other letters to lowercase.
  PROPER(Textvalue)

- Repeat text in text value.
  REPEAT(Textvalue, Count)

- Replace characters.
  Offset,Length, Newtext)
  REPLACE(Oldtext,

- Right-most characters from Text value
  RIGHT(Textvalue, Length)

- Give text entry in first cell of range as
  text. Returns blank text if cell contains 0.
  S(RangeReference)

- Give value converted to number
  with specified number of decimal
  places.
  STRING(x, Decimalplaces)

- Remove blank spaces from text.
  TRIM(Textvalue)

- Convert text to uppercase.
  UPPER(Textvalue)

- Convert text to number.
  VALUE(Textvalue)

268

INDEX

3-D

A

B

C

(continued...)

INDEX (continued)

(continued...)

INDEX (continued)

(continued...)

INDEX (continued)

(continued...)

272

(continued...)

INDEX (continued)

(continued...)

274

INDEX (continued)

(continued...)

INDEX (continued)

(continued...)

INDEX (continued)

N

O

P

(continued...)

INDEX (continued)

(continued...)

INDEX (continued)

(continued...)

INDEX (continued)

(continued...)

INDEX (continued)

(continued...)

INDEX (continued)

FREE CATALOG
&
UPDATED LISTING

We don't just have books that find your answers faster; we also have books that teach you how to use your computer without the fairy tales and the gobbledygook.

We also have books to improve your typing, spelling and punctuation.

Tear out the slip below and return it to us for a free catalog and mailing list update.

RETURN TODAY!

- -

14 E. 38th St. New York, NY 10016

❑ Please send me your catalog and put me on your mailing list.

_____
Name

_____
Firm (if any)

_____
Address

_____
City, State, Zip

More Quick Reference Guides

	Cat. No.		Cat. No.
Access 1.1 Windows	MA-18	OS/2 2.1	Y-18
Ami Pro 3 Windows	Z-18	PageMaker 5(IBM/Macintosh)	PM-18
cc:Mail 2.0 Windows	CC18	Prodigy	P-18
Computer Terms	D-18	Quattro Pro 4 (DOS)	Q-18
dBase III Plus (DOS)	B-17	Quattro Pro 5 Windows	0-QPW5
dBase IV (DOS)	B-18	Quicken 6 (DOS)	QB-17
DOS 5	J-17	Quicken 7 (DOS)	0-QK7
DOS 6	R-18	Quicken 2 Windows	C-18
Excel 4 Windows	A-18	Quicken 3 Windows	0-QKW3
Excel 5 Windows	F-18	UNIX	U-17
Excel 4 Macintosh	G-18	Windows 3.1	N3-17
Lotus 1-2-3 (DOS) Release 2.2	L2-17	Windows NT	NT-18
Lotus 1-2-3 (DOS) Release 2.3	L-18	Windows for Workgroups	WG-18
Lotus 1-2-3 (DOS) Release 2.4	K-18	Word 5.0 Macintosh	T-17
Lotus 1-2-3 (DOS) Release 3.1	J-18	Word 5.5 (DOS)	E-17
Lotus 1-2-3 (DOS) Release 3.4	L3-17	Word 2.0 Windows	WN-17
Lotus 1-2-3 Windows Rel. 1.1	LW-17	Word 6.0 Windows	0-WDW6
MS Works 2 (DOS)	K-17	WordPerfect 5.1 (DOS)	W-5.1
MS Works 2 Windows	H-18	WordPerfect 6.0 (DOS)	W-18
MS Works 3 Windows	0-WKW3	WordPerfect Windows 5.1/5.2	Z-17
MS Works 3 (DOS)	M-18	WordPerfect Windows 6.0	0-WPW6